Test Yourself

By Jack Shafer

**Drawings by
Rowena Huber**

1975 EDITION

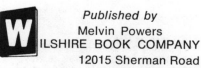
Published by
Melvin Powers
WILSHIRE BOOK COMPANY
12015 Sherman Road
No. Hollywood, California 91605
Telephone: (213) 875-1711

Printed by

HAL LEIGHTON PRINTING CO.
P.O. Box 1231
Beverly Hills, California 90213
Telephone: (213) 983-1105

ISBN 0-87980-259-6

CONTENTS

INTRODUCTION

It's always fun to find out what a person is *really* like—especially when that person is yourself! Here is your chance to find out!

Have you ever noticed that you like to do the things you are best at? As you glance through the tests and quizzes your eyes will probably light up at certain categories as you say to yourself, "That's duck soup!" But don't skip the tests that look hard, or those you think you know nothing about, for that's where the biggest surprises may lie! Each of us has hidden talents which should be discovered and encouraged.

Some of the quizzes on which you encounter difficulty may help you discover just where you go wrong and help you to get on the right track. Others will simply point out fields for which you have no particular natural aptitude. It's as important to recognize your limitations as your talents so that you don't end up a square peg in a round hole.

Don't expect these tests to serve as a magic crystal ball, but they will tell you a lot about yourself if you follow the directions faithfully. Write your answers on a separate sheet of paper (don't write in the book or you may spoil someone else's fun), or better still, write them in a notebook and date them. Then you can take the tests over again at a future time and see what progress you have made, or how much you have remembered!

WORD MEMORY TEST—No. 1

There are eight simple words in each of the following four columns. Work with one column at a time. Read the column *aloud,* and try to repeat the words in correct order mentally; then read the column aloud again. Immediately close the book and proceed to write as many of the words as you can remember, preferably (but not necessarily) in their original order.

After you have finished all four columns, compare your lists with the originals.

street	boy	hat	salt
light	desk	coat	pepper
lamp	school	shirt	stove
pole	chalk	shoes	pan
bank	blackboard	tie	water
clock	words	rack	sink
night	book	closet	faucet
policeman	teacher	door	drip

(For scoring, see page 88.)

WORD MEMORY TEST—No. 2

Follow the same directions as for the previous test.

house	auto	farm	railroad
roof	wheels	cow	track
walls	gears	pig	switch
doors	tires	horse	locomotive
windows	hood	crop	cars
basement	lights	land	signal
path	ignition	wires	station
gate	keys	phone	gates

WORD MEMORY TEST—No. 3

Follow the same directions as for the previous tests.

bread	flax	fringe	privilege
landscape	skunk	school	restaurant
staff	bridge	tree	sky
plate	tooth	banister	frenzy
marmoset	ice	coffee	temptation
town	skin	temperature	cliff
chair	plow	aspic	joke
brush	train	space	rival

(For scoring, see page 88.)

AUDITORY MEMORY TEST

Read the following passage *aloud* three times, allowing a short interval between each reading to memorize the major points or ideas contained in it. Allow another half minute after the third reading. Then write down on a sheet of paper as many of the major points or ideas as you can remember.

If a sailor
is shipwrecked
on the ocean
and reaches shore alone
in a wild country
he should first look for water to drink
then find a safe place to sleep
where wild animals can't get at him
afterward he can look for food
being suspicious of strange berries or fruits
then he had better hunt for people on the land
and get a large fire ready
to signal ships that might pass.

(For scoring, see page 88.)

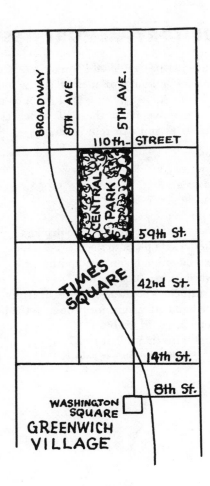

MAP MEMORY TEST—No. 1

Study this map for 2 minutes and try to memorize it. Then close the book and draw the map from memory, complete with street names, as well as you can. Allow 2 minutes to draw the map, then stop.

(For scoring, see page 89.)

MAP MEMORY TEST—No. 2

Study this map for 3 minutes. Make no notes. It is not carefully drawn, but it shows the position of the countries involved. Now shut the book and draw the map from memory, outlining the countries and filling in the names to the best of your ability. Allow 3 minutes.

(For scoring, see page 89.)

VISUAL AND AUDITORY MEMORY TEST

Study the picture, then read the following passage aloud three times, allowing a short interval between each reading to memorize the major points or ideas contained in it. Allow another ½ minute after the third reading. Then write down on a separate paper as many of the major points or ideas as you can remember.

This is a strange looking railroad station
because it is in the Orient
Trains come into it from the north and the south
They are often late
There is a large waiting room on the second floor
Poor people often sleep there all night
The station attendants all speak English
But there are no Englishmen among them
The station was built in 1912
It is of mixed architecture
Steam locomotives have blackened it
Its walls have never been cleaned.

(For scoring, see page 90.)

VISUAL DESIGN TEST—No. 1

Take both of these tests before consulting the scoring section in order to get a good idea of your artistic and visual memory.

Study the design for this test for only 10 seconds. Then close the book and immediately draw the design on a separate sheet of paper, as accurately and carefully as you can, freehand. Allow 1 minute. Then proceed to the following test.

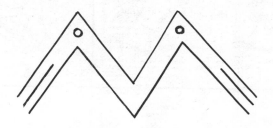

VISUAL DESIGN TEST—No. 2

Follow the same directions as for the previous test, except that you may study this design for 20 seconds.

(For scoring, see pages 90 and 91.)

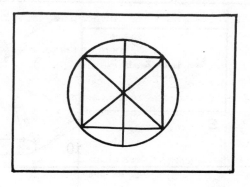

ARTISTIC PERCEPTION TEST

In each of the following pictures one vital detail is missing. On a separate sheet of paper list the missing items by number. Allow 3 minutes.

(For scoring, see page 91.)

1.

2.

3.

4.

5.

6.

7.

8.

9.

10.

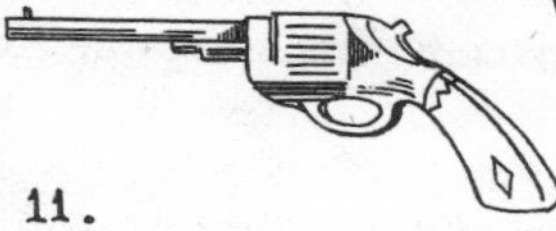

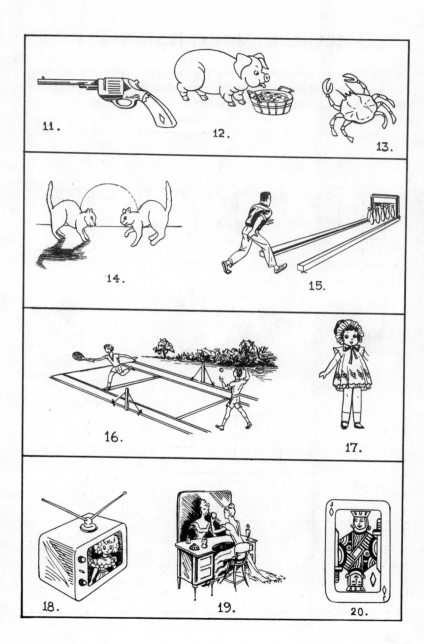

11.

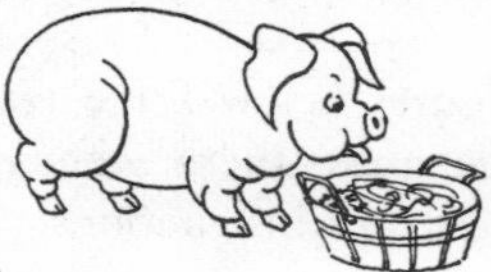

12.

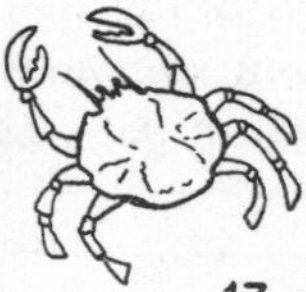

13.

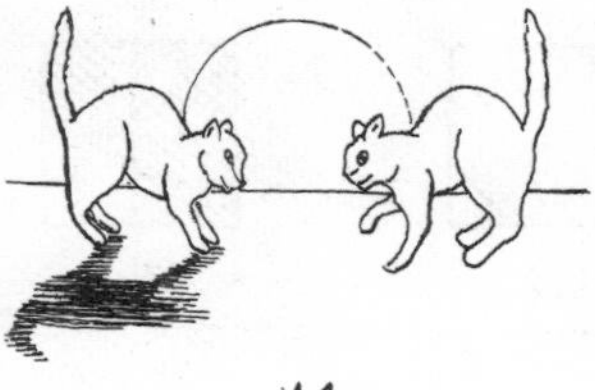

14.

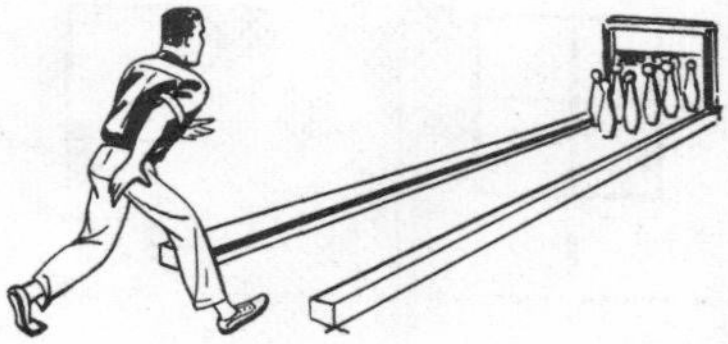

15.

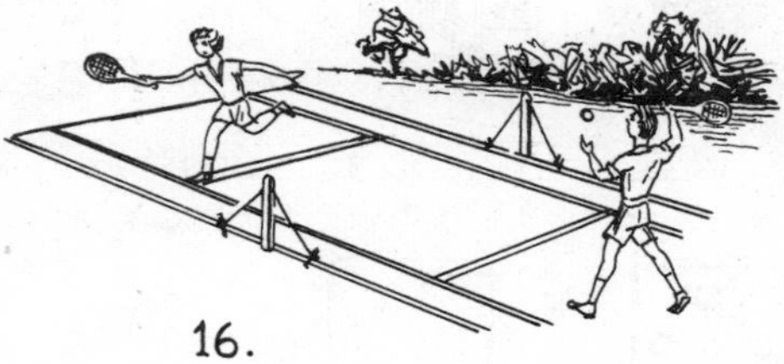

16.

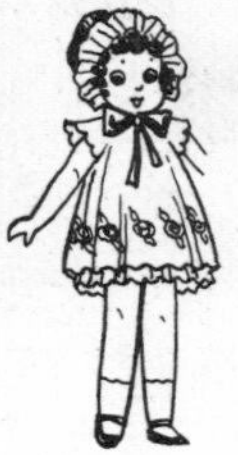

17.

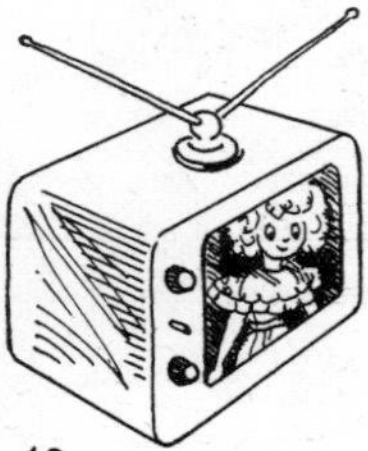

18.

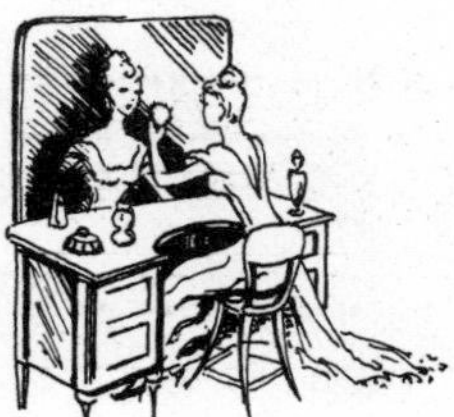

19.

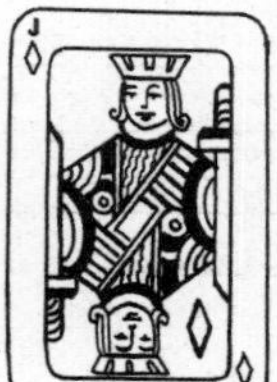

20.

VISUAL MEMORY TEST—No. 1

Study the 10 figures below for 2 minutes, trying to remember them so you will recognize them when you see them again. Now turn to page 92 for further instructions.

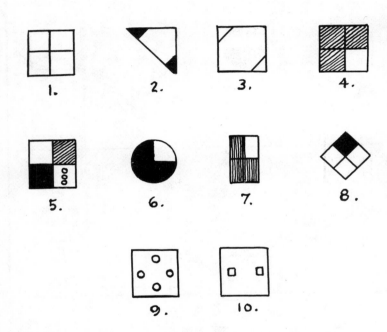

VISUAL MEMORY TEST—No. 2

Follow the same directions as for the previous test, then turn to page 93.

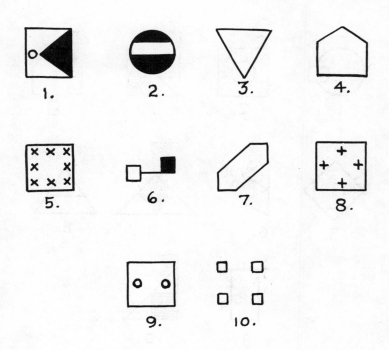

VISUAL MEMORY TEST—No. 3

Follow the same directions as for the previous test, then turn to page 94.

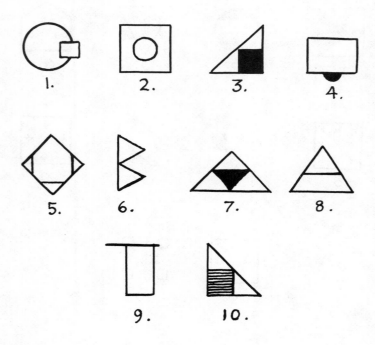

1.   2.   3.   4.

5.   6.   7.   8.

9.   10.

NAME MEMORY TEST

Read the following passage *aloud,* just once. Try to remember the names of persons, things, colors, etc., that are mentioned in it. Have a pencil and a sheet of paper ready, but make no notes. Then immediately turn to page 95 and answer the questions there.

Last night Bert Schafer, a foreman, met two of his best workers, Tim Mallon and Bill Tanner, coming out of a restaurant. Tim Mallon was carrying a red flag with green letters that read "Black for President." Bill Tanner carried a yellow flag with green letters that read "Gray for Vice President."

Bert asked them what the banners were all about. They explained they were coming from a meeting of their fraternal order, The Serene Eagles, where a rally had just been held for a forthcoming election of officers, to be held next Saturday.

CROSSLINE MEMORY TEST—No. 1

Study the following figure to determine the relationships of the numbers. Allow yourself one minute. Then close the book and on a separate piece of paper draw the complete figure from memory. Allow only 15 seconds for this second step. Then check for accuracy.

There is no scoring page for this test. Four tests of increasing difficulty are provided. Proceed from the first test to the last, allowing 1 minute to study each test and 15 seconds to reproduce it. Failure to complete any test within the time limit indicates deficient number comprehension and memory.

NO. 1

NO. 2

CROSSLINE MEMORY TEST—No. 2

Follow the same instructions as for the previous test.

6	0	5
7	0	6
8	0	7
9	0	8

CROSSLINE MEMORY TEST—No. 3

Follow the same instructions as for the previous tests.

2	8	4	5
3	12	6	7
4	16	8	9
5	20	10	11
6	24	12	13

CROSSLINE MEMORY TEST—No. 4

Follow the same instructions as for the previous tests.

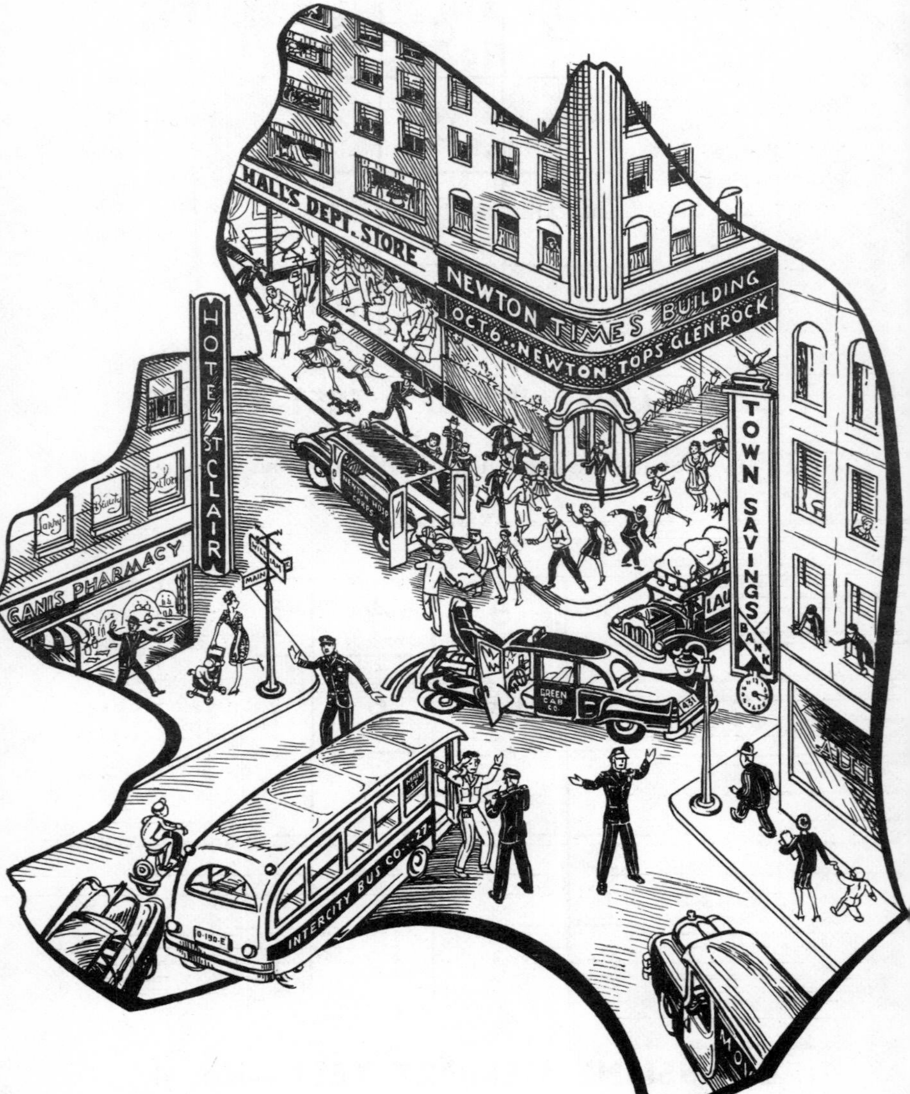
HALL'S DEPT. STORE
NEWTON TIMES BUILDING
OCT. 6 · NEWTON TOPS GLEN ROCK
HOTEL ST CLAIR
TOWN SAVINGS BANK
GANIS PHARMACY
INTERCITY BUS CO. 27
GREEN CAB CO.
MAIN

OBSERVATION AND MEMORY TEST
No. 1

To test your ability to perceive and remember details well, study the picture on page 20 for 2 minutes. Make only mental (no written) notes. Then turn to page 95 and answer the questions there without referring back to the picture.

OBSERVATION AND MEMORY TEST
No. 2

Study the picture on the next page for 5 minutes, but make no written notes. Then close the book and on a separate sheet of paper write down as many items as you remember from the scene. (Don't break any single item into its component parts, such as table top, table legs, etc. That's simply one item, a table.) Then turn to page 96 for a list of items appearing in the drawing.

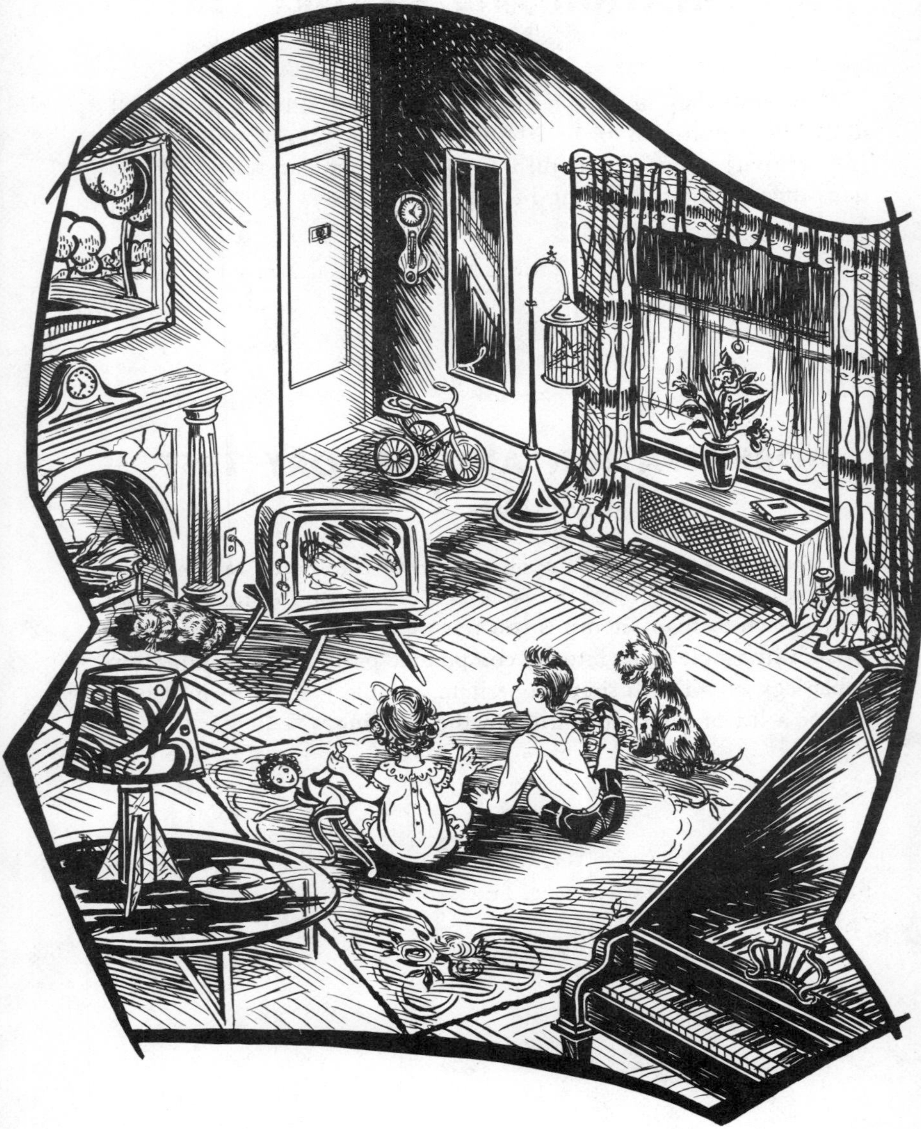

REASONING TEST—No. 1

Time yourself on this test. Allow 2½ minutes to write your answers on a sheet of paper. Don't spend excessive time on any one question. If you don't get it promptly, go on to the next. Only on this basis can accurate scoring results be made.

1. If 2 pencils can be bought for 5 cents, how many pencils can be bought for 50 cents?

2. A motor boat was rented by a man and his wife, his two daughters and their husbands, and three children in each daughter's family. How many were in the boat?

3. What is the well-known proverb which expresses the idea that a person who is prompt usually derives an advantage over tardy people?

4. In the following series, two pairs are wrong. Rewrite the series correctly.

$$2\ 5 \qquad 3\ 6 \qquad 5\ 9 \qquad 1\ 4 \qquad 6\ 8$$

5. The moon bears a relationship to the earth as the earth bears a relationship to what body of our solar system?

6. If a strip of cloth 36 inches in length shrinks to 32 inches after washing, how long will a strip of the same cloth, originally 45 inches, be after washing?

7. Count each S in the following series that is followed by an R provided the R is not followed by an A. How many such S's are there?

A R S R T O S R A S R S G S R Y D S R A

8. If a rope 24 feet long is cut so that the shorter piece is one-half as long as the other piece, how many feet long will the shorter piece be?

(For scoring, see page 97.)

REASONING TEST—No. 2

Follow the same instructions as for the previous test.

1. One number is wrong in the following series. Write the series correctly.

$$4 \quad 8 \quad 16 \quad 32 \quad 65 \quad 128$$

2. One number is wrong in the following series. Write the series correctly.

$$2 \quad 4 \quad 15 \quad 256 \quad 65{,}536$$

3. If a man runs 100 yards in 10 seconds, how many *feet* does he run in 1 second?

4. Freezing water bursts pipes because:

    (a)—the cold weakens the pipes
    (b)—the ice stops circulation of the water
    (c)—water expands when it freezes

5. If the earth were nearer the sun:

    (a)—the stars would become invisible
    (b)—our months would be longer
    (c)—the earth would become warmer

6. It is colder nearer the poles than at the equator because:

    (a)—there is more ice at the poles
    (b)—the poles are further from the sun
    (c)—the sun shines more obliquely at the poles

7. If a man wanted to give away a million dollars, he would do the most good by:

    (a)—giving it to the government toward the national debt
    (b)—giving it to various worthy charities
    (c)—giving it all to some poor person

8. What well-known saying expresses the thought that children get frivolous in school when the teacher is absent?

(For scoring, see page 97.)

REASONING TEST—No. 3

Follow the same instructions as for Reasoning Test No. 1.

1. If an argument or difference of views is settled by mutual concession, it is called:

> (a)—restraint; (b)—injunction; (c)—compromise; (d)—deadlock.

2. What his neighbors and friends say about a man constitutes:

> (a)—his character; (b)—his personality; (c) his outlook; (d)—his reputation; (e)—his psyche.

3. The ohm is used in measuring:

> (a)—electricity; (b)—water power; (c)—rainfall; (d)—wind velocity.

4. Give the two numbers that should come at the end of each of these series of numbers:

8	1		6	1		4	1		_	_
81	27		27	9		9	3		3	1	_ _

5. Supply the words that will make this a clear sentence:

> It is usually very —— to become ——— with people who are ——— timid.

6. Do the same with this sentence:

> A reasonable ——— of sleep is usually ——— if a person is to ——— a high ——— of efficiency.

7. A submarine makes 20 miles an hour underwater and 30 miles an hour on the surface. How long will it take to cross a 150-mile channel if it has to go 3/5ths of the way on the surface?

8. A contest of any sort always has:

> (a)—an umpire; (b)—an audience; (c)—ticket takers; (d)—opponents; (e)—victory.

(For scoring, see page 97.)

WORD RELATIONSHIP TEST—No. 1

In each of the following groups of four words, pick the word which *least* belongs there. Allow one minute to list your answers on a separate sheet of paper. (For scoring, see page 98.)

1. breakfast, grapefruit, dinner, supper
2. cow, horse, dog, tiger
3. book, magazine, newspaper, letter
4. recline, rest, sleep, slumber
5. forest, woods, grove, tree
6. hen, goose, duck, swan
7. Albany, New York, Texas, Alaska
8. shout, cry, whimper, yell
9. slippers, stockings, boots, shoes
10. view, landscape, scenery, picture
11. Venus, Earth, Mars, Sun
12. gloaming, twilight, evening, dawn

WORD RELATIONSHIP TEST—No. 2

In each of the following groups of four words, pick the word which *least* belongs there. Allow two minutes to list your answers on a sheet of paper. (For scoring, see page 99.)

1. marsh, morass, quagmire, atoll
2. zephyr, typhoon, current, breeze
3. docile, tractable, cordial, grudging
4. paragon, perfection, sound, sprung
5. remedy, curare, antidote, physic
6. hydrogen, oxygen, carbon, water
7. Sirius, Arcturus, Tauri, Castor
8. Guernsey, Hereford, Shorthorns, Civet
9. ulna, biceps, triceps, deltoid
10. tibia, femur, fibula, pelvis
11. Mohammed, Moses, Darwin, Buddha
12. parishioner, minister, prelate, pontiff

CAUSE AND EFFECT TEST

The idea of this test is to pick a word that is the *effect* of each of the following *cause* words. For example, "shipwreck" is a logical effect word to follow "storm."

On a separate sheet of paper, write the most logical effect word you can think of for each of the following cause words. Allow yourself two minutes. (For scoring, see page 99.)

1. nourishment
2. melting snows
3. hunger
4. dirt
5. exercise
6. effort
7. cold

8. injury
9. crime
10. work
11. practice
12. beauty
13. debt
14. piano

POWER TO INTERPRET TEST

There are 7 numbered proverbs on the left side of this page, and 14 lettered statements on the right. Each proverb has close application to 2 of the statements from the right-hand column. For example, "Every cloud has a silver lining" has a close relationship to statement (b), "It is a long lane that has no turning," as well as to one other statement.

On a separate sheet of paper list numbers 1 through 7, then match up two letters, (a) through (n), for each number.

1. He counsels best who lives best.

2. Anyone can hold the helm when the sea is calm.

(a) Wisdom is often nearer when we stoop than when we fly.

(b) It is a long lane that has no turning.

(c) Learn and profit by the mistakes of others.

3. Every cloud has a silver lining.

4. More is obtained from one book carefully read than from libraries skimmed with a wandering eye.

5. He is truly wise who gains wisdom from another's mishaps.

6. Cowards die many times before their death.

7. As for me, all I know is that I know nothing.

(d) They who fear too much suffer more than those who die.

(e) Jack of all trades, master of none.

(f) Untempted virtue is easiest to keep.

(g) Concentrate your energies for best results.

(h) It's an ill wind that blows no good.

(i) Learn to see in another's calamity the ills you should avoid.

(j) A good example is the best sermon.

(k) An unassaulted castle is easily defended.

(l) Practice what you preach.

(m) The valiant never taste of death but once.

(n) The doorstep to the temple of wisdom is a knowledge of our own ignorance.

(For scoring, see page 100.)

NUMBER RELATIONSHIP TEST—No. 1

The numbers in each of the left-hand series below follow a definite "rule" or pattern. You are to determine this numerical relationship or rule. Then from among the numbers to the right you are to choose the one number which correctly continues the series. For example:

10 11 13 14 16 17   17 18 19 20 22   Answer: 19

Studying the left-hand numbers we discover that the "rule" here is to add 1 then add 2, add 1, add 2, etc. Therefore we now must add 2 to 17 and the answer is 19. Another illustration:

4 6 9 13 18 24   26 27 29 31 33   Answer: 31

The rule here is add 2, add 3, add 4, etc.

Study these illustrations till you understand the numerical principles involved. Then, on a separate sheet of paper, write down your answers to the following problems. Allow 2 minutes.

A.	31	33	31	34	31	35	30	31	34	35	40
B.	5	5	5	3	3	3	0	1	2	3	4
C.	7	9	11	13	11	9	7	9	11	13	15
D.	12	36	18	18	54	27	18	27	36	54	81
E.	21	22	20	23	19	24	16	18	25	29	30
F.	3	6	12	21	24	30	32	36	39	60	99

(For scoring, see page 100.)

NUMBER RELATIONSHIP TEST—No. 2

See the explanation and instructions in the preceding test. Allow 2 minutes.

A.	1	2	3	1	2	3	0	1	2	3	4
B.	90	45	50	25	30	15	0	5	15	20	10
C.	22	25	28	31	34	37	38	39	40	41	42
D.	72	36	40	20	24	12	16	4	8	12	16	20
E.	5	10	7	14	11	22	19	16	20	24	32	38
F.	95	92	46	42	21	16	8	2	4	6	8	10

(For scoring, see page 101.)

NUMBER RELATIONSHIP TEST—No. 3

See the explanation and instructions for previous tests. Allow 2 minutes.

A.	24	27	9	18	21	7	14	11	17	22	28	33
B.	44	40	42	14	10	12	4	0	2	6	7	10
C.	3	6	5	5	8	7	7	6	7	10	13	14
D.	1	2	5	11	12	15	21	22	24	25	27	30
E.	14	16	13	17	12	18	11	15	16	17	18	19
F.	9	10	8	24	6	7	5	3	6	15	16	20

(For scoring, see page 101.)

NUMBER RELATIONSHIP TEST—No. 4

See the explanation and instructions for previous tests. Allow 2 minutes.

A.	76	38	36	18	16	8	6	1	2	3	4	5
B.	81	27	54	18	36	12	24	4	8	21	24	48
C.	90	82	74	66	58	50	42	32	34	36	38	40
D.	21	20	22	20	23	20	24	16	20	24	28	29
E.	6	9	7	10	8	11	9	7	10	12	13	14
F.	8	10	12	10	12	14	12	10	12	14	16	18

(For scoring, see page 101.)

WORD RELATIONSHIP AND GENERAL KNOWLEDGE TEST—No. 1

This is a two-fold test, as its name implies. Each scrambled sentence includes all the words needed to make a comprehensive statement. Some statements, when unscrambled, are true; some are false. On a separate sheet of paper write down the unscrambled statements and mark each one true or false. Allow 5 minutes.

1. gotten sea water sugar is from
2. every times makes mistakes person at
3. rated razor as barber's once medical tool a the
4. a device for pressure measuring the of atmosphere barometer is the
5. Belleau where was Woods Germans the stopped the U. S. Marines World War I in
6. wheat the crops minor Soviet Russia one is of of
7. avenues of Marseille Champs Elysees the is of one main the
8. English Channel in the a group of islands the Islands Channel are
9. is a cloud detached delicate of appearance cloud the cirrus
10. cheetah the attain speed a of miles 100 per hour can animals among the
11. primitive to people a small on living island a place small the seems world
12. of Asia southern and eastern in tea chiefly hilly is grown countries

(For scoring, see page 102.)

WORD RELATIONSHIP AND GENERAL KNOWLEDGE TEST—No. 2

See the instructions for the preceding test.

1. common use in aluminum lightest the metal is

2. point is 100 degrees in scale the Fahrenheit water of boiling the

3. except hydrogen lightest gas for helium is the

4. established by Louis Pasteur bacteria was to disease the relation of

5. western in America the bighorn species is a found of buffalo

6. leg the human of important bones the femur are and tibia fibula

7. played the Kirk van Gogh movies in the part of Douglas Vincent

8. railroad was built locomotive successful by the first Robert Fulton

9. an oily pitch black coal tar from bituminous coal distilled is

10. the pole star living to one at north the pole directly always would overhead be

11. compounds acids are hydrogen containing and a non-metallic element

12. revolution during the French an unimportant Jacobins the were party political

(For scoring, see page 103.)

MATHEMATICAL JUDGMENT TEST—No. 1

Don't try to figure out these examples exactly. The time element won't allow it, and the test is not for accuracy but judgment. Your arithmetic reasoning power will determine how well you do at approximating the right answer to these problems. There are 4 possible answers for each problem. Working quickly, write down on a separate sheet of paper the answers that seem most likely to be right. Allow 2½ minutes.

1. A man left ⅓ of his net estate to charity and ½ of the remainder went to each of his children. If each child got $10,000, what was the total of his net estate?

<blockquote>$20,000 $140,000 $30,000 $70,000</blockquote>

2. A factory employs 200 women, 150 single men and 650 married men. If each group is expanded proportionately until there are 1150 total employees, how many additional women will be hired?

<blockquote>13 1100 30 563</blockquote>

3. If you buy 5 pens at $.25 each and 12 ornamental weights at $2.00 a dozen, what will the total cost be?

<blockquote>$1.10 $4.96 $3.25 $15.00</blockquote>

4. A dealer marked some goods at $.60 a yard but sold them at a 20% discount and still made a profit of 20% of the cost. What was the cost of the goods per yard to the dealer?

<blockquote>$.12 $1.30 $.40 $.08</blockquote>

5. Based on her average time, a typist can type a page in 3½ minutes. How many pages can she copy in 98 minutes?

<blockquote>6 19 160 28</blockquote>

(For scoring, see page 104.)

MATHEMATICAL JUDGMENT TEST—No. 2

See explanation for previous test.

1. If 3½ tons of coke cost $42, what will 7½ tons cost?

$50. $120. $90. $175.

2. If it takes 16 barrels of oil at $2.50 per barrel to process one-half a mile of road, how much will it cost for five miles of road?

$400. $1300. $875. $260.

3. A girl worked Monday through Friday from 9:00 to 5:00 with 45 minutes out for lunch each day. How many hours and minutes did she work that week?

40 hours 30 minutes   42 hours
30 hours 30 minutes   36 hours 15 minutes

4. A company's total expenses last year were $450,000. Its sales expenses for the period were $36,900. What percentage was sales expense of total expense?

8.2%   12.7%   33⅓%   19.0%

5. To combine like fractions in algebra, we add or subtract their numerators as indicated by their signs, write the result over the common denominator, then reduce the fraction to lowest terms. Two problems (a) and (b) follow. Which problem and solution are correct?

(a) Combine $\dfrac{3r}{6} - \dfrac{2r}{6} + \dfrac{r}{6}$

Solution: $\dfrac{3r - 2r + 6}{3r}$

Or $2\frac{1}{3} r$

(b) Combine $\dfrac{5}{4x} + \dfrac{9}{4x} - \dfrac{8}{4x}$

Solution: $\dfrac{5 + 9 - 8}{4x}$

Or $\dfrac{6}{4x}$ or $\dfrac{3}{2x}$

(For scoring, see page 104.)

MATHEMATICAL JUDGMENT TEST—No. 3

See explanation on page 33.

1. If a food loses 20% of its weight in processing, how many pounds of it must be bought in its raw state to produce 800 pounds when processed?

1000   1460   1300   812

2. Five telephone poles are placed along a street 40 yards apart. How many yards is the first pole from the last?

200   1240   186   160

3. Two automobiles start toward each other from opposite ends of a highway which is 105 miles long. If one auto travels at 30 miles an hour average and the other at 40 miles an hour average, how many hours will it be before they meet?

12    $\frac{1}{2}$ $3\frac{1}{2}$ $1\frac{1}{2}$

4. A square courtyard would contain 81 square yards if each of its present sides were lengthened by 3 yards. How many yards long is each side at present?

10   14   6   9

5. A square courtyard would contain 81 square yards *more* if each of its present sides were lengthened by 3 yards. How many yards long is each side at present?

3   12   40   27

(For scoring, see page 104.)

MECHANICAL COMPREHENSION TEST
No. 1

Examine each picture intently for not more than ten seconds. Then answer the question for it, without looking at the picture again. Proceed through all five pictures before consulting the answers.

1. Assume that A and B are wooden balls suspended in such a way that they just touch each other when at rest. If A is drawn aside and let fall against B, B will be thrust to the right. Will A bounce back an equal distance, or will it be brought to rest by the impact?

2. Under which jacket will the snow melt faster?

3. Which parachute will reach the earth first?

4. Assuming that C is the power shaft, will shaft A or shaft B turn faster?

5. Notice the direction in which the drive wheel moves. Does gear C move in the direction of the arrow marked "A" or the arrow marked "B"?

(For scoring, see page 104.)

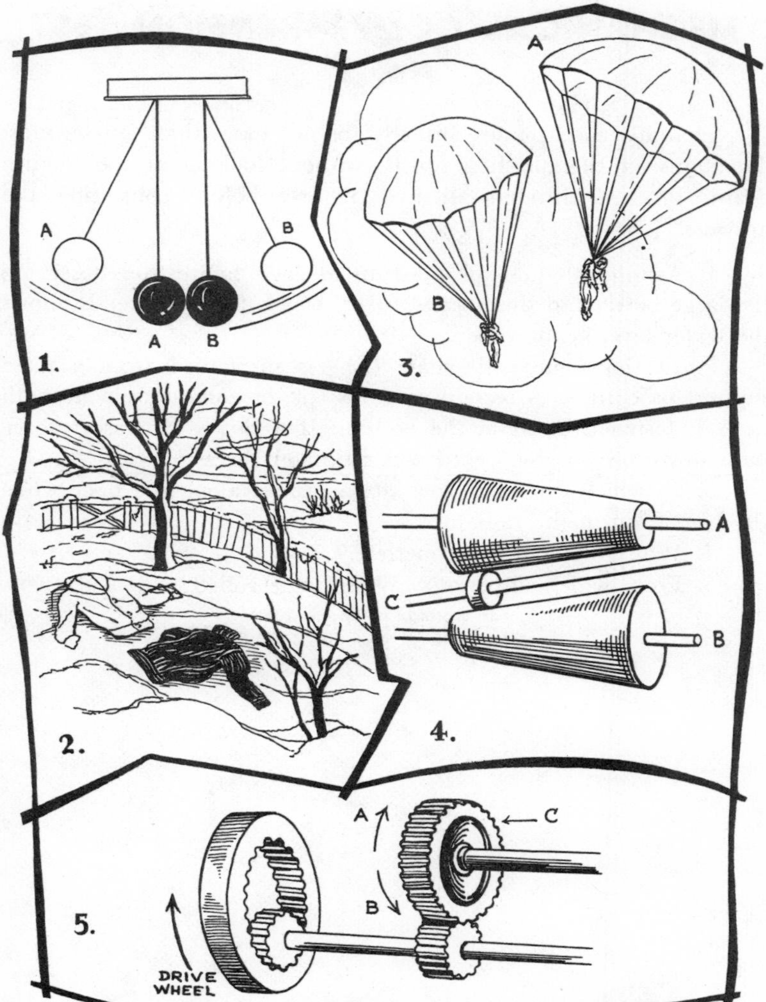
A
B
A
B
1.
A
B
3.
2.
A
C
B
4.
A
C
B
5.
DRIVE
WHEEL

MECHANICAL COMPREHENSION TEST
No. 2

Examine each picture intently for not more than ten seconds. Then answer the question for it, without looking at the picture again. Proceed through all five pictures before consulting the answers.

1. Assuming equal air pressure in each figure and observing the large bowls and the narrow tubes, which figure correctly shows the water level in the tube?

2. In this figure, the mass (M) is suspended from a fixed support by cord A. A second cord (B) of the same tensile strength as A is fastened to M at the bottom. If a slowly increasing force pulls down on B, which cord will ultimately break?

3. In which direction does the air move along the floor when the heat is on in the radiator?

4. Which will cut metal better?

5. From which direction was the table rolled?

(For scoring, see page 105.)

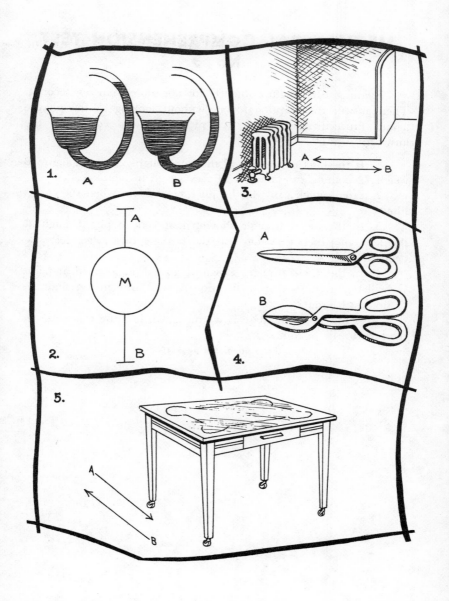

1. A   B

3. A ←   → B

2. A   M   B

4. A   B

5. A → B

MECHANICAL COMPREHENSION TEST
No. 3

Examine each picture intently for not more than ten seconds. Then answer the question for it, without looking at the picture again. Proceed through all five pictures before consulting the answers.

1. If the tank of water and the iron weight shown in figure B weigh 72 pounds, how much will they weigh in figure A?

2. From which can will the juice pour faster when the can is tilted?

3. In the metal triangle shown, if an axle is put through at point O, in which direction will the triangle turn when left suspended?

4. In the metal triangle shown, if an axle is inserted at point O, will the triangle turn in direction A or B, or will it remain in motionless balance?

5. If the air in the flask is warmed, will it cause the water in the tube to rise or fall?

(For scoring, see page 105.)

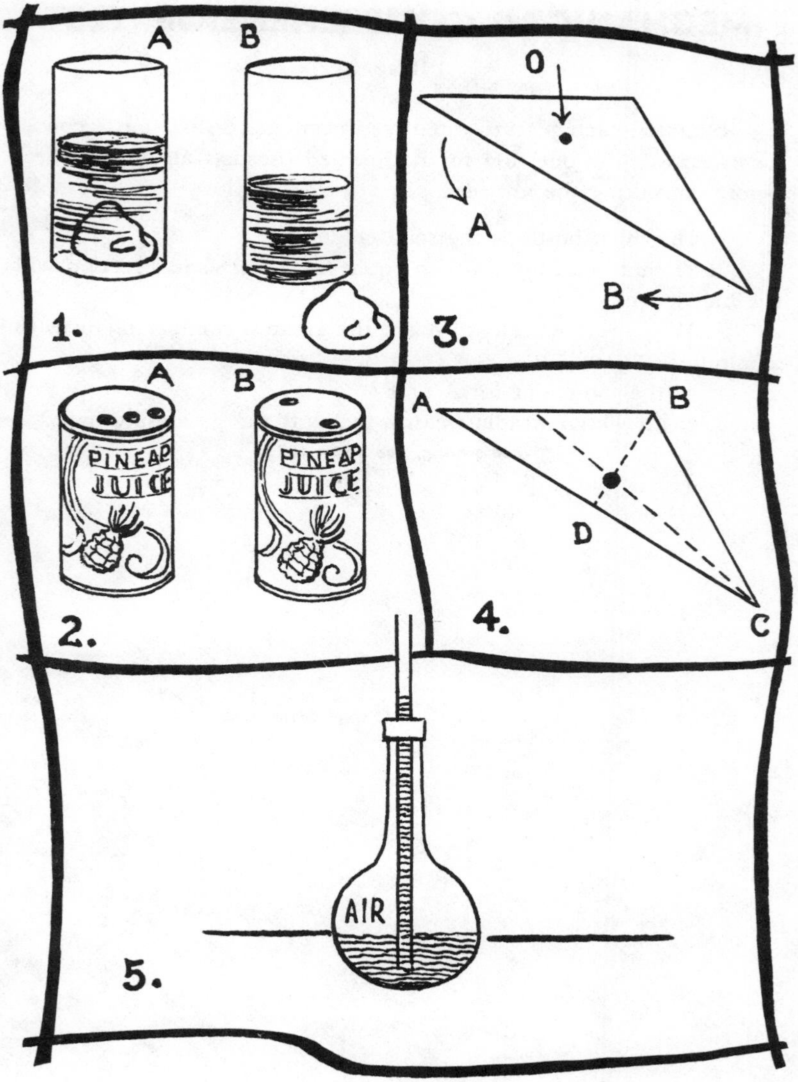
A
B
1.
O
A
B
3.
A
B
PINEAP
JUICE
PINEAP
JUICE
2.
A
B
D
4.
C
AIR
5.

MECHANICAL COMPREHENSION TEST
No. 4

Examine each picture intently for not more than ten seconds. Then answer the question for it. Proceed through all five pictures before consulting the answers.

1. In which bottle is the soda colder?

2. If each man pushes with equal force, in what direction will the ball move?

3. What gear wheel will make the greatest number of turns in a minute?

4. Is the job easier for A or B?

5. With which windlass can a man lift the greatest weight?

(For scoring, see page 105.)

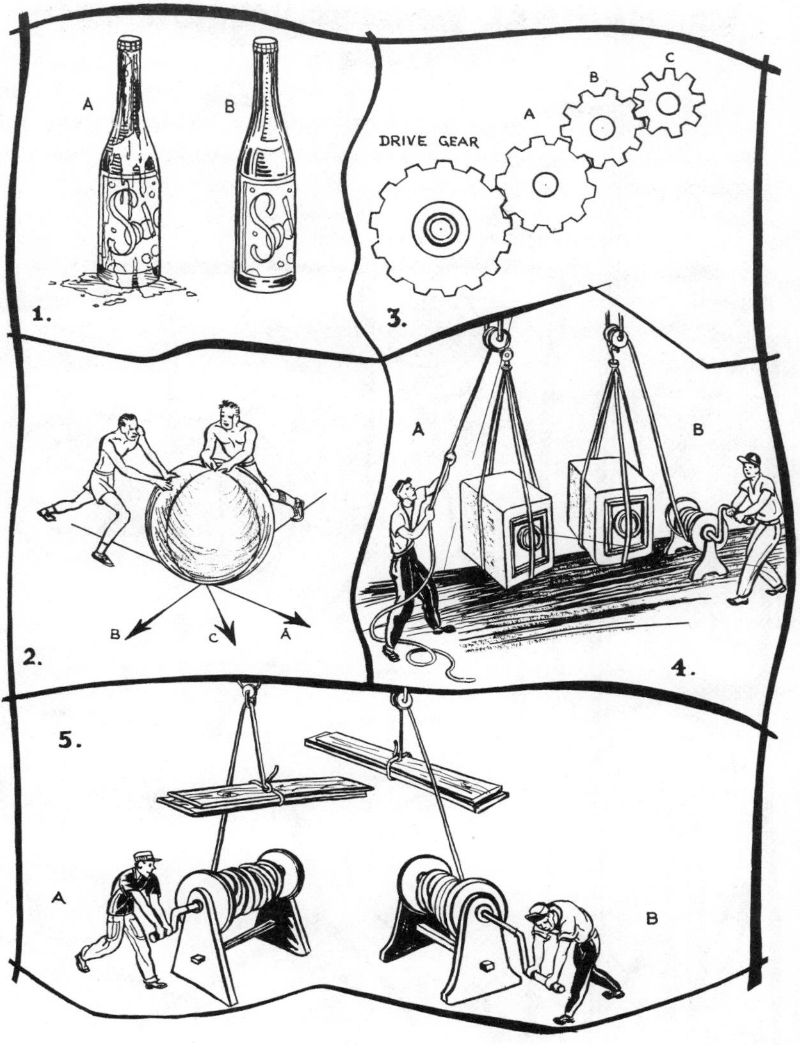
1.
A
B
3.
DRIVE GEAR
A
B
C
2.
B
C
A
4.
A
B
5.
A
B

MECHANICAL TOOL COMPREHENSION
TEST—No. 1

Part of a person's mechanical aptitude is reflected by his familiarity with tools. Try to pair off the following 8 drawings of tools or parts of tools within 1 minute.

(For scoring, see page 106.)

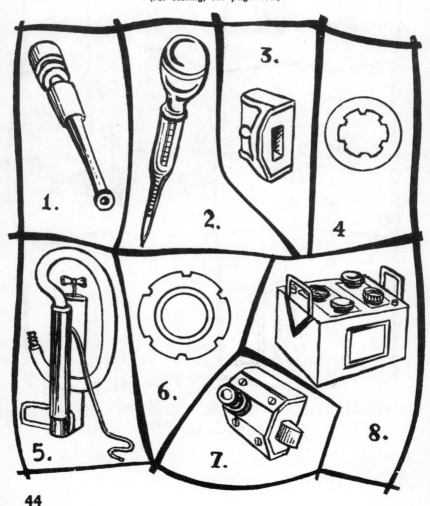

1.

2.

3.

4.

5.

6.

7.

8.

MECHANICAL TOOL COMPREHENSION
TEST—No. 2

Follow the directions for the previous test.

(For scoring, see page 106.)

WORD POWER TEST—No. 1

Each of the following definitions stands for a word whose initial is among the letters below it. For example:

An iced area used for skating.

A T R O W C

"R" is the letter, for the appropriate word, of course, is "rink."

Allow 1 minute to do as many as you can of the following 6 problems.

1. An excessive rate of interest.

T O P U C B

2. A formal relinquishment of governmental power.

P I M S A L

3. An agreeable, compatible combination of tones.

H J D E I Q

4. A dish made of eggs and milk.

L P M O K H

5. Furiously hungry.

T N V C S R

6. A favorite pursuit, aside from one's occupation.

J L E H S A

(For scoring, see page 106.)

WORD POWER TEST—No. 2

See instructions for the previous test.

1. A fabled sea creature with a woman's body and a fish's tail.

H O M S U E

2. A period of time without beginning or end.

J C F E I A

3. A recluse from society.

B H D S F W

4. The claw of an eagle.

G O P J T B

5. A place for keeping food cold.

T H E O P R

6. A periodic payment of money for services rendered.

S D Y K B C

(For scoring, see page 106.)

WORD POWER TEST—No. 3

See instructions for previous tests.

1. A space completely devoid of matter.

D G V O Y T

2. The artificial watering of land to provide crops with moisture.

R I E W C L

3. A shadow drawing.

S P M V C D

4. The element which, combined with oxygen, forms water.

A I R P H K

5. The doctrine that the chief pursuit of life is pleasure.

J S N W X H

6. Inability to obtain required sleep.

I T R O N B

(For scoring, see page 107.)

WORD MEANING TEST—No. 1

The idea of this test is to select, from a group of words, a word that means either *the same as* or *the opposite of* the key word given. For example:

Deep: ocean   shallow   thoughtful   useful

The key word is deep and the answer is shallow—in this case the opposite of deep.

Write down on a separate sheet of paper the word you think is correct in each of the following 8 cases. Allow no more than 10 seconds for each part.

1. Gradual: brisk, elevated, inward, sudden
2. Vapid: insipid, obedient, hopeful, stubborn
3. Seemly: fragile, poetic, interested, fit
4. Devout: worshipped, strong, impious, penitant
5. Contemptible: unable, corrupt, despicable, somber
6. Energetic: sensitive, virtuous, apathetic, heroic
7. Gaunt: haggard, unhappy, prosaic, insipid
8. Eternal: vigilant, sky, changeless, temporary

(For scoring, see page 107.)

WORD MEANING TEST—No. 2

Follow instructions for the previous test.

1. Envious: covetous, snide, possessive, unhappy
2. Reserved: studious, dumb, reticent, ticket
3. Identical: heterogeneous, alien, close, distant
4. Moderate: modern, slow, temper, extreme
5. Romantic: youth, male, silent, prosaic
6. Liberal: sublime, generous, lavish, party
7. Round: soft, large, circular, ellipse
8. Cruel: vicious, hasty, angry, modest

(For scoring, see page 107.)

WORD RELATIONSHIP TEST—No. 3

In the following series there are two key words, related in a way which you will have to determine. Next a problem word is given, followed by four optional words. From those four words pick the one which has the same relationship to the problem word as in the key words. For example:

	Problem	
Key Words	Word	Words to Choose From
Cattle: hay	man: ?	eat, drink, bread, dessert

The answer, of course, is "bread." Now try the following problems, writing your answers on a separate sheet of paper. Allow 10 seconds for each.

1. Clock: watch   trunk: ? suitcase, train, redcap, taxi
2. Phone: hear   telescope: ? distance, enemy, seek, see
3. Author: book   sculptor: ? artist, clay, stone, statue
4. Horse: carriage locomotive: ? track, steam, coal, cars
5. Illness: crisis drama: ? stage, ticket, climax, act
6. Best: quality   most: ? goods, income, quantity, produce
7. Crowd: people   herd: ? dog, cows, silo, barn
8. Past: future   history: ? prophet, dictator, army, prediction

(For scoring, see page 108.)

WORD RELATIONSHIP TEST—No. 4

For instructions, see previous test.

	Problem	
Key Words	Word	Words to Choose From
1. Fang: lion	thorn: ?	stick, hurt, rose, injure
2. Battle: duel	chorus: ?	duet, song, choir, orchestra
3. Disease: cleanliness	accident: ?	hospital, doctor, caution, insurance
4. Portrait: painter	symphony: ?	opera, conductor, cello, orchestra
5. Water: thirst	air: ?	hydrogen, oxygen, suffocation, life

6. Yard: space   hour: ? time, clock, year, calendar
7. Imitate: create   copy: ? picture, originate, learn, depend
8. Arm: elbow   leg: ? skin, foot, bursa, knee

(For scoring, see page 108.)

SPEED OF IMAGINATION TEST—No. 1

Suppose that overnight the entire world supply of oil vanished so far into the earth as to be irrecoverable. How many *important* changes do you think this catastrophe would produce in the entire world? Thinking and writing as fast as you can, list as many changes as you can imagine. Allow 1 minute. Write only the key words, such as:

1. Change distribution of wealth.
2. Produce fuel crisis, etc.

Be sure you stop writing at the end of 1 minute.

(For scoring, see page 108.)

SPEED OF IMAGINATION TEST—No. 2

Suppose that an awful plague swept the world (as the Bubonic plague did centuries ago) and killed or severely disabled 40% of the general population. How many *important* changes would this catastrophe produce in your town or city? List them on a separate sheet of paper. Think and write as fast as you can, writing only the key words of your thoughts.

Be sure you stop at the end of 1 minute.

(For scoring, see page 109.)

CONSTRUCTIVE IMAGINATION TEST
No. 1

Note: Take both of these tests, one after the other, before consulting the scoring device on page 110. This will give you a truer test of your imaginative powers.

Suppose that atomic energy is developed to the point where it is the cheapest and most practical way to provide the world with heat and light. The fuel needed to run a big city an entire week would weigh only a few pounds. However, huge quantities of uranium would have to be processed at isolated atomic energy plants.

Without explanations, write down as many important ways as you can think of in which this change would affect the commerce of the world. Allow 2 minutes.

CONSTRUCTIVE IMAGINATION TEST
No. 2

Think of the station in life you can reasonably hope to attain by the end of the next ten years. How successful can you expect to be? What sort of a job can you anticipate holding, etc.?

With that idea pretty well defined in your mind, now write down whatever practical suggestions you think you might well follow in order to attain your ten-year goal.

Allow 3 minutes for this test. Keep your ideas within practical range—nothing like, "Hope my rich aunt will die."

(For scoring, see page 110.)

CONSTRUCTIVE IMAGINATION TEST
No. 3

Imagination is not just the faculty of thinking of something new. Applying present knowledge and experience to the solution of a new problem involves imagination—the process of putting toward new usage the things we already know.

One dependable test for constructive imagination is the composition of familiar words from a limited number of letters. This is such a test.

Allow yourself 3 minutes to construct familiar words (no names) from the letters. Don't repeat a letter in any word.

T S A R I O E Y
(For scoring, see page 110.)

CONSTRUCTIVE IMAGINATION TEST
No. 4

Make up as many words as you can from the following six letters. Names don't count. Don't use the same letter more than once in any word. No other letter may be used. Stop at the end of 5 minutes.

A E I L P R
(For scoring, see page 110.)

CREATIVE IMAGINATION TEST—No. 1

Many liquid products come in beautifully designed bottles which are good for more than just their initial use. How many of the following additional uses could such a bottle be employed for? ANY DEGREE OF USEFULNESS IS ACCEPTABLE.

1. toy
2. lamp base
3. door stop
4. weapon
5. bookend

6. ornament
7. float
8. liquid container
9. candle base
10. musical instrument

(For scoring, see page 111.)

CREATIVE IMAGINATION TEST—No. 2

We all know the conventional use of each of the items listed below. Your job is to think of some *unconventional* use for each item which would have some measure of practical value under ordinary or unusual circumstances. Allow 3 minutes.

1. hammer
2. nail
3. pencil
4. hairpin
5. coin

6. newspaper
7. lampshade
8. inkwell
9. circular doily
10. lady's large straw handbag

(For scoring, see page 111.)

CREATIVE IMAGINATION TEST—No. 3

In the following list of familiar household appliances, think of some improvement not presently contained in conventional models. This improvement can be far fetched as long as it has *some* utilitarian value. In other words, use your imagination freely. Allow ten minutes for this test.

1. food mixer
2. radio
3. washing machine
4. vacuum cleaner
5. toaster
6. refrigerator
7. steam iron
8. floor polisher
9. television set
10. electric alarm clock

(For scoring, see page 112.)

CREATIVE IMAGINATION TEST—No. 4

The pictures below have reference to famous nursery tales. See if you can figure out appropriate *titles* for each picture by drawing on your knowledge of nursery tales. Allow 2 minutes.

(For scoring, see page 113.)

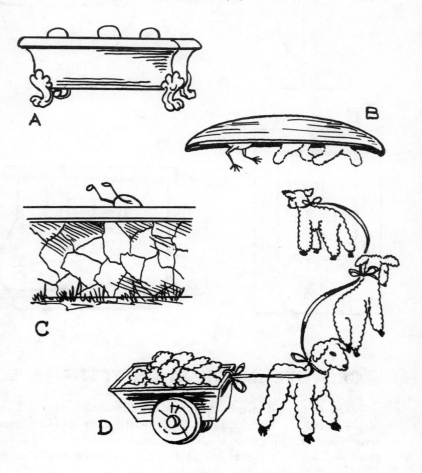

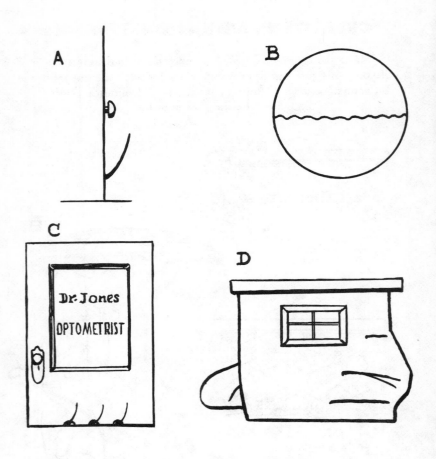

CREATIVE IMAGINATION TEST—No. 5

The pictures drawn on this page are incomplete in that some of the detail has been omitted. Nevertheless, each should suggest some scene or figure to you. Allow yourself 3 minutes to see if you can come up with the artist's identification of these 4 figures, or ones you think are just as applicable.

(For scoring, see page 113.)

CONCENTRATION TEST—No. 1

Concentration is the ability to disregard other matters and focus attention on a particular task. It is essential to constructive thinking. Try to take the following 4 tests under something other than ideal conditions. Have the radio going, the TV set on, or provide some other distraction.

In each line of numbers below you will find one or more pairs of adjacent numbers whose sum is 10. List by line the pairs you can find within 3 minutes.

(a) 4 1 8 4 9 1 3 0 4 8 5 9 6 8 4 7 6 9 4 0 1 3 2 8 3 7 5 4 4 8
(b) 9 8 6 4 3 8 5 8 1 3 8 5 6 7 0 9 4 8 2 3 1 5 8 7 4 0 9 8 6 1
(c) 3 1 8 6 0 3 9 4 1 2 3 7 0 4 8 6 9 0 5 1 2 8 5 0 9 9 4 8 6 7
(d) 7 5 5 0 1 2 8 4 8 9 8 1 5 8 4 8 7 3 9 1 5 8 4 7 6 9 4 1 3 2
(e) 6 2 4 8 3 4 0 9 2 8 4 3 8 5 1 3 8 4 8 6 7 4 1 8 3 7 9 8 0 4
(f) 6 9 3 8 1 3 5 6 7 8 3 4 5 7 8 3 7 5 7 2 9 4 3 1 2 9 4 3 8 6
(g) 8 5 9 4 8 3 7 4 9 8 1 3 8 7 4 1 8 2 0 7 4 6 5 1 4 7 5 5 6 3
(h) 5 3 4 7 6 3 5 9 8 2 3 7 6 6 3 0 1 4 6 2 2 5 7 9 3 4 2 3 8 5
(i) 4 9 3 9 6 3 0 3 6 8 5 5 8 9 1 4 0 8 6 7 6 3 4 7 2 9 5 8 3 5
(j) 1 1 9 2 7 5 1 6 8 7 4 5 6 1 3 9 2 4 3 6 7 4 8 4 3 9 5 6 9 9

(For scoring, see page 113.)

CONCENTRATION TEST—No. 2

The idea here is to subtract (mentally) a series of 7's from 100 until no further subtraction can be made. As you make the mental subtractions, call them off orally to a person who is following the scoring on page 114.

Allow only 45 seconds. If you make a mistake, the person helping you is to correct you immediately. Continue your subtractions *from that point* correctly.

An excellent result is secured if you complete the series within 45 seconds without making more than 1 mistake.

CONCENTRATION TEST—No. 3

The idea of this test is to subtract mentally first 1's, then 2's alternately from the number 50. As you make the mental subtractions, call them off orally to a person who is following the scoring on page 114.

Only 45 seconds are allowed. If you make a mistake, the person helping you is to correct you *immediately*. Continue subtractions *from that point* correctly.

An excellent result is secured if you complete the subtractions within 45 seconds without making more than one mistake.

CONCENTRATION TEST—No. 4

In each of the ten lines of letters below you will find one or more combinations of consecutive letters which spell words in common usage. On a separate sheet of paper list the words that you find, line by line. When you put together the words from each group of letters, they should form a meaningful sentence.

Allow 3 minutes.

1. P T A O C I F N I J R Q T S E J L I U V T E W H X O L P Y O U

2. F R L D O J V U L H Q R C W E L L V X A G L T E F T H E Y R C

3. C M I U V N T X E Z B J M I N O R V H G I T A S K S M J E J X

4. W H I C H A Q E V F R T I Y T H L D Y O U C N I J R N E Z E F

5. D L E Q G H T S V X A R E Z U I O C A L L E D E T J Q V N I R

6. X N I Q J E V K F F I H R D L J I Q H U I Y I H T L R U P O N

7. T O Q L R T S D E V H P E R F O R M I D X V Y O U M T Q W Z Z

8. B R W I L L L J A Q H A V E W J H G B U T R J I A L I T T L E

9. E O C J D I F F I C U L T Y R D W I T H C J R Q A K S H L D U

10. V J B I Q T H E I U B J L I H V B I G G E R B L O N E S R Z X

(For scoring, see page 114.)

ACCURACY TEST—No. 1

The paired columns of numbers below consist of some exact duplicates and some which differ slightly. Working quickly but as accurately as possible, jot down on a separate sheet of paper the key numbers of those pairs which are *the same*.

Allow 1½ minutes only, and if you cannot finish in the allotted time, note the number at which you stop.

1.	650	650	14.	36015992	360155992
2.	041	044	15.	3910066482	391006482
3.	2579	2579	16.	8510273301	8510273301
4.	3281	3281	17.	263136996	263136996
5.	55190	55102	18.	451152903	451152903
6.	39190	39190	19.	3259016275	3295016725
7.	658049	650849	20.	582039144	582039144
8.	3295017	3290517	21.	61558529	61588529
9.	63015991	63019991	22.	211915883	219915883
10.	39007106	39007106	23.	670413822	670143822
11.	69931087	69931087	24.	17198591	17198591
12.	251004818	251004418	25.	36482991	36482991
13.	299056013	299056013			

(For scoring, see page 115.)

ACCURACY TEST—No. 2

Follow the same directions given for the previous test.

1. 10243586	10243586	14. 3484657120	3484657210
2. 659012534	659021354	15. 8588172556	8581722556
3. 388172902	381872902	16. 3120166671	3120166671
4. 631027594	631027594	17. 7611348879	76111345879
5. 2499901354	2499901534	18. 26557239164	26557239164
6. 2261059310	2261659310	19. 8819002341	8819002341
7. 2911038227	2911038227	20. 6571018034	6571018034
8. 313377752	313377752	21. 38779762514	38779765214
9. 1012938567	1012938567	22. 39008126557	39008126657
10. 7166220988	7162220988	23. 75658100398	75658100398
11. 3177628449	3177682449	24. 41181900726	41181900726
12. 468672663	468672663	25. 6543920817	6543920871
13. 9104529003	9194529003		

(For scoring, see page 115.)

(For scoring, see page 115.)

THOROUGHNESS TEST—No. 1

Thoroughness consists of attention to detail and accuracy in following specific directions. Study the figure below briefly. The lower part of the page contains questions that you are to answer, referring to the figure whenever necessary. Work rapidly, since there is a 2-minute time limit, but remember you are aiming for thoroughness. Write your answers on a separate sheet of paper.

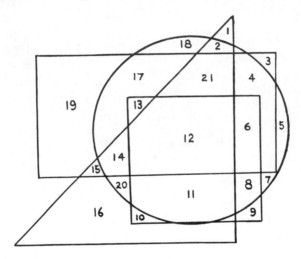

What numbers are:

1. In the triangle but not in the square, circle or rectangle?
2. In the circle but not in the square, triangle, or rectangle?
3. In the square but not in the circle, triangle, or rectangle?
4. In the rectangle but not in the circle, triangle, or square?
5. In both triangle and circle but not in the square or rectangle?
6. In both circle and square but not in the rectangle or triangle?
7. In both square and triangle but not in the rectangle or circle?

(For scoring, see page 115.)

THOROUGHNESS TEST—No. 2

Referring to the diagram in the preceding test and following the same instructions, answer the following questions in 2 minutes:

What numbers are:

1. In both triangle and rectangle but not in the square or circle?

2. In both circle and rectangle but not in the square or triangle?

3. In rectangle and triangle and circle but not in the square?

4. In rectangle and circle and square but not in the triangle?

5. In triangle and square and circle but not in the rectangle?

6. In rectangle and square and triangle but not in the circle?

7. In rectangle and square and triangle and circle?

(For scoring, see page 116.)

ORGANIZING ABILITY TEST—No. 1

In each of the boxes below you are shown geometrical pieces that can be fitted into a perfect square. On a separate piece of paper draw these shapes so that you form a square from each set of pieces. If you can readily visualize and then form the component parts into a whole, you're a good organizer. Allow 5 minutes.

(For scoring, see page 116.)

1

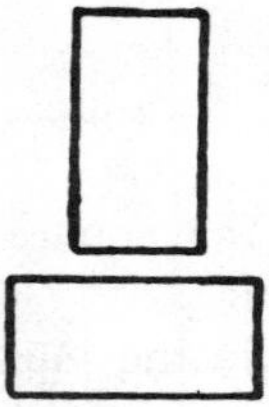

2

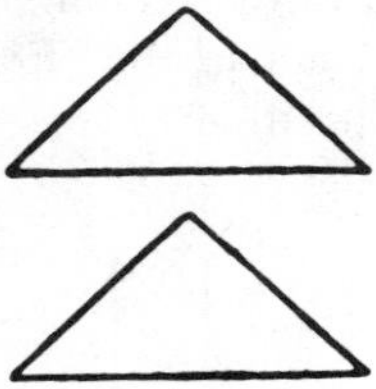

3

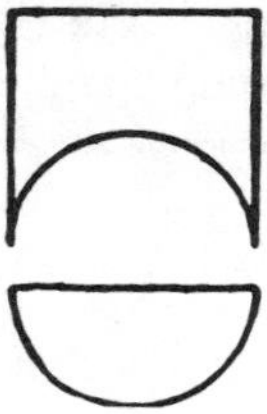

4

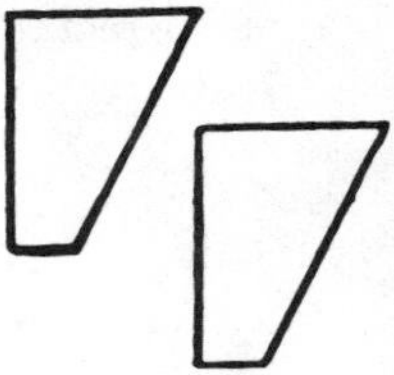

5

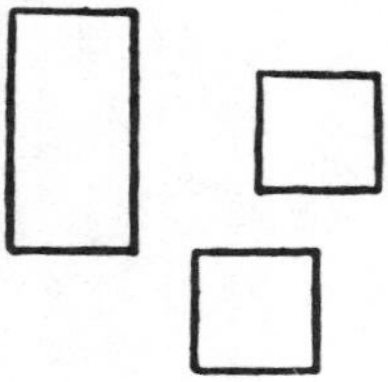

6

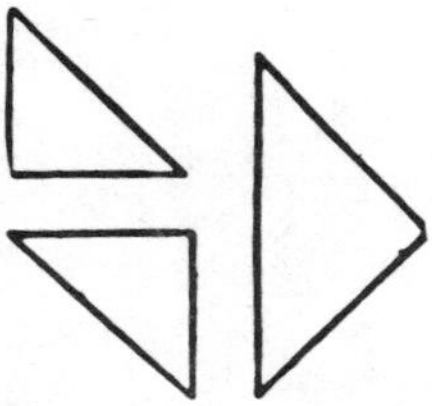

7

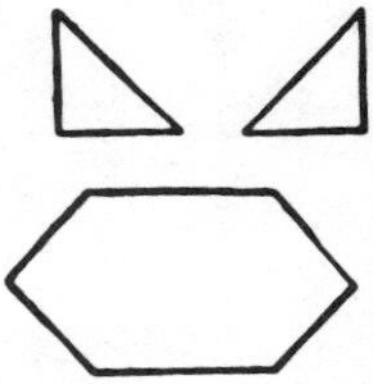

8

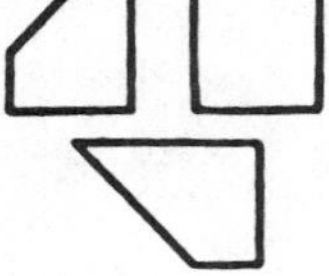

9

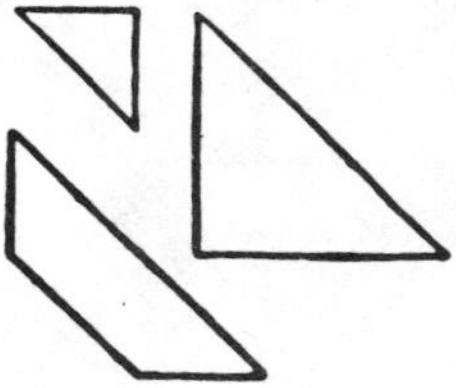

10

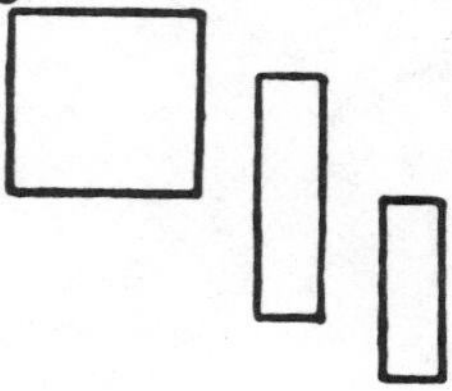

ORGANIZING ABILITY TEST—No. 2

Follow instructions for previous test, but allow 4 minutes.
(For scoring, see page 117.)

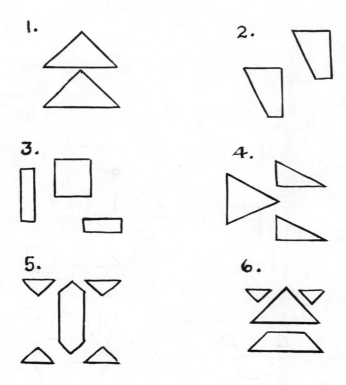

ORGANIZING ABILITY TEST—No. 3

This test is almost the same as the 2 previous tests, except that here you are required to fit the component parts into varying shapes, as indicated for each problem. Allow 5 minutes.

(For scoring, see page 118.)

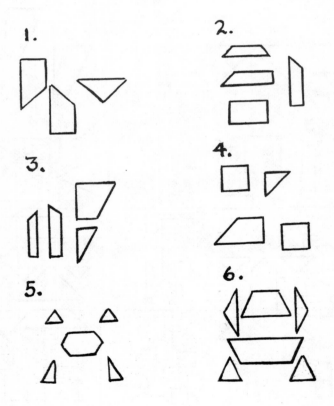

VISUALIZATION TEST

The first rows of the following piles of cubes show you how many cubes are contained in each pile. Study them to understand how the sum is arrived at, then figure out the number of cubes contained in each of the piles below. You may use any method of calculation and you may make notes on paper. Allow 3 minutes.

(For scoring, see page 118.)

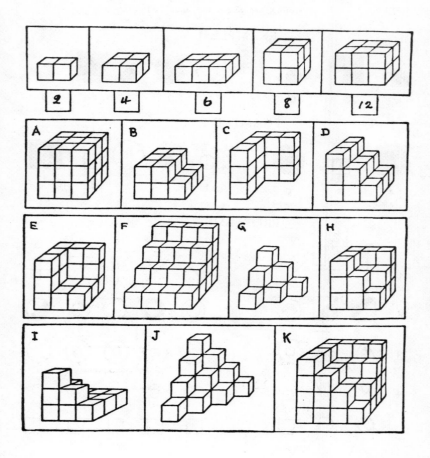

VISUAL ANALYSIS TEST—No. 1

To analyze the problems below you must ask yourself, "A is to B as C is to what?" For instance, in the first example below B is the same as A, only larger, so you would choose figure 2 (from among the 5 optional figures) for your answer. In Example 2 the answer is 1, the same shape but smaller and hollow. When you think you understand the examples, proceed to the test below. Allow 2 minutes to jot the answers down on a separate sheet of paper. **(For scoring, see pages 119 and 120.)**

EXAMPLE 1

EXAMPLE 2

PROBLEMS

VISUAL ANALYSIS TEST—No. 2

Follow instructions for the preceding test.

(For scoring, see page 120.)

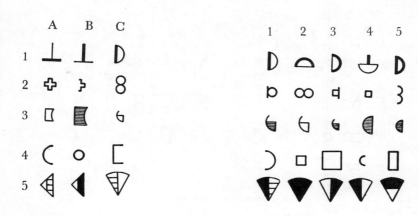

VISUAL ANALYSIS TEST—No. 3

Follow instructions for the preceding test.

(For scoring, see page 120.)

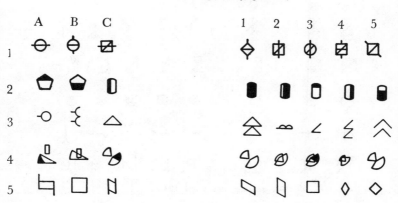

VISUAL ANALYSIS TEST—No. 4

See the instructions for Visual Analysis Test—No. 1. Then proceed with the following ten figure examples. Allow five minutes.

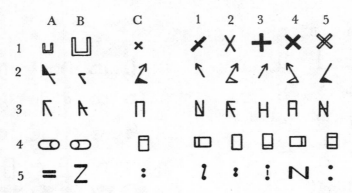

(For scoring, see page 120.)

VISUAL ANALYSIS TEST—No. 5

See instructions for Visual Analysis Test—No. 1.

(For scoring, see page 121.)

PATTERN VISUALIZATION TESTS

The following tests (8 in all) are based on patterns that can be folded into solid forms. Without actually cutting out and folding the patterns, study the figure on the left in each test and decide which figures of those on the right of the line could be made from the pattern figure. Sometimes more than 1 correct figure is shown. Then, on a separate sheet of paper list the answers for all 8 tests before consulting the scoring page. Allow time as marked.

TEST—No. 1 (Allow 2 minutes)

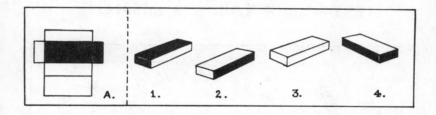

TEST—No. 2 (Allow 2 minutes)

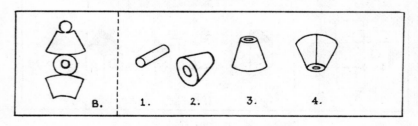

(For scoring, see page 121.)

TEST—No. 3 (Allow 3 minutes)

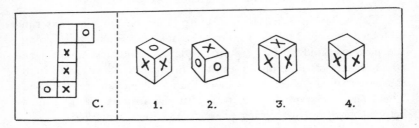

TEST—No. 4 (Allow 3 minutes)

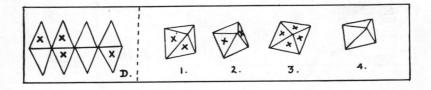

TEST—No. 5 (Allow 3 minutes)

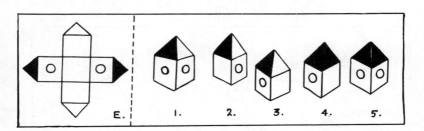

(For scoring, see page 121.)

TEST—No. 6 (Allow 3 minutes)

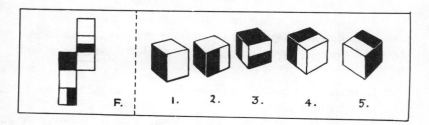

TEST—No. 7 (Allow 3 minutes)

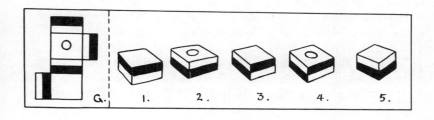

TEST—No. 8 (Allow 2 minutes)

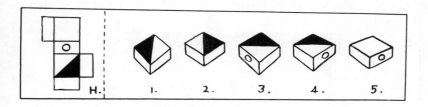

(For scoring, see page 121.)

SPACE PERCEPTION TEST

There is no time limit on this test, but don't use a pencil or any other device to figure out the answers. Just use your imagination and mental perception to judge or guess at the answers and write them on a sheet of paper.

1. What is the width, in inches, between two railroad tracks of standard gauge?

2. If you held the figure 124 up before a mirror what would it look like?

3. A clock reads 11:45. If you changed the small hand for the large hand and the large hand for the small hand, what time would it show?

4. Imagine that you fold a square sheet of paper in half, then fold it in half again. Now imagine that you take an office paper punch and punch it once through the folded paper. Now "unfold" the paper. How many punched holes will there be in it?

5. Assume that you fold a square sheet of paper once on the diagonal, then fold it again so it forms a triangle, then punch a hole through the folded sheet. Now "unfold" it. How many holes?

6. What is the length in inches of a row of 20 ordinary size postage stamps?

7. What is the diameter in inches of a regulation size basketball?

8. A clock reads 5 minutes after 3. Exchange the hands. Now what time does it show?

9. How many inches wide is the standard size newspaper page (not the tabloid)?

10. What would the abbreviation "&" look like if held up to a mirror?

(For scoring, see page 121.)

PRECISION TEST—No. 1

The idea in these tests is to replace familiar digits with unfamiliar symbols. Each number from 1 to 9 is represented by a symbol, thus:

1	2	3	4	5	6	7	8	9
–	И	⊐	L	U	O	∧	×	=

You may study the above symbols for a few minutes. Now, on a separate sheet of paper copy the two lines of numbers below. Allow yourself 2½ minutes to write the correct symbol below each digit. You may, of course, keep the book open in front of you.

1 5 4 2 7 6 3 5 7 2 8 5 4 6 3 7 2 8 1 9 5 8 4 7 3

6 2 5 1 9 2 8 3 7 4 6 5 9 4 8 3 7 2 6 1 5 4 6 3 7

(For scoring, see page 122.)

PRECISION TEST—No. 2

See the instructions for the preceding test. However, do all three rows on this page as quickly as you can, instead of observing a specific time limit. Time yourself carefully to determine how many seconds it takes you to complete the 3 rows.

1	2	3	4	5	6	7	8	9
—	И	Ⴑ	L	U	O	∧	✕	＝

3 1 2 1 3 2 1 4 2 3 5 2 9 1 4

6 3 1 5 4 2 7 6 3 8 7 2 9 5 4

6 3 7 2 8 1 9 5 8 4 7 3 6 9 5

(For scoring, see page 122.)

PRECISION TEST—No. 3

Follow the instructions for Precision Test—No. 2.

1	2	3	4	5	6	7	8	9
—	И	Ⴑ	L	U	O	∧	✕	＝

1 9 2 8 3 7 4 6 5 9 4 8 5 7 6

9 3 8 6 4 1 5 7 2 6 2 4 8 1 3

4 9 5 1 7 5 2 6 9 3 7 8 4 1 8

(For scoring, see page 123.)

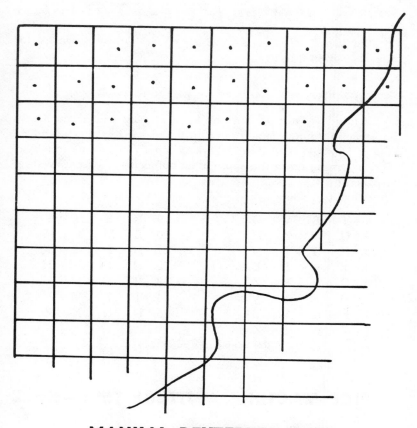

MANUAL DEXTERITY TEST

Rule a sheet of paper into 150 half-inch squares (10 squares by 15).

With a sharp pencil held lightly in writing position, tap a dot within each square. Go from left to right in the top column, then from right to left in the second column, from left to right in the third, etc. Don't stop to correct errors. Try to work as rapidly as possible and still retain accuracy.

Allow only 30 seconds.

(For scoring, see page 123.)

OFFICE MACHINE APTITUDE TEST—No. 1

Study the following Key which gives a letter as symbol for each digit from 0 to 9:

0	1	2	3	4	5	6	7	8	9
E	H	G	V	N	Y	T	F	W	Z

Below are listed 15 lines of 4 letters each which you are to transpose into numbers according to the above Key. For example: W F Y V would be 8 7 5 3. Work as rapidly but as accurately as possible writing down the appropriate numbers on a separate sheet of paper.

Allow ½ minute.

1.	T	E	V	G	9.	N	E	H	Y
2.	G	W	Z	H	10.	E	V	T	H
3.	H	T	F	N	11.	H	F	H	T
4.	V	N	H	E	12.	H	G	V	H
5.	G	F	E	Z	13.	Y	G	V	Y
6.	H	N	E	V	14.	T	Z	V	Y
7.	F	H	V	G	15.	N	H	N	Z
8.	Y	W	E	Z					

(For scoring, see page 124.)

OFFICE MACHINE APTITUDE TEST—No. 2

Follow the directions for the previous test.

1.	H	N	W	G	9.	V	T	Z	H
2.	H	E	V	N	10.	F	N	Y	T
3.	H	V	Y	V	11.	N	G	T	F
4.	G	V	Z	Y	12.	T	V	E	N
5.	H	Y	W	Y	13.	W	G	V	F
6.	Y	E	Z	G	14.	Y	Z	V	E
7.	N	Z	E	N	15.	F	G	N	V
8.	Y	W	E	H					

(For scoring, see page 124.)

COPYREADING APTITUDE TEST—No. 1

The lists below consist of 15 pairs of names. On some lines the names are exactly alike. On some lines slight differences or errors appear. On a separate sheet of paper list by number the lines containing one or more errors.

Allow 40 seconds for the test.

1. Sheppard Novelty Co.	Shepard Novelty Co.
2. Roberts and Lennon, Inc.	Roberts and Lennen, Inc.
3. Joseph Pape and Sons	Joseph Pape and Sons
4. Thompson Co.	Thompson, Inc.
5. Simplex Shoe Corp.	Simplex Shoe Corp.
6. Leibster & Bros.	Liebster & Bros.
7. Silver Standards Co.	Silver Standard Co.
8. Oppenheimer and Powers	Oppenheimer and Powers
9. Powers and Oppenheimers	Power and Oppenheimers
10. Northern Texas Petroleum	No. Texas Petroleum
11. Royaltone Corporation	Royalton Corporation
12. G. H. Furnath Co. Inc.	G. H. Furnath Co. Inc.
13. Harold Jacobsohn Co.	Herald Jacobsohn Co.
14. Terrell Express Co.	Terrill Express Co.
15. Hart Wallder and Sons	Hart Wallder and Sons

(For scoring, see page 124.)

COPYREADING APTITUDE TEST—No. 2

Follow the same instructions for the preceding test.

1. Knappe and Johns	Knapp and Johns
2. Greenland Masonite Products	Greenland Masonit Products
3. Magic Seal Supplies	Magic Seal Supply
4. Seton Hall College	Setan Hall College
5. Imperial Coats, Inc.	Imperial Coats, Inc.
6. Shagmoor Furs Co.	Shagmore Furs Co.
7. Personnel Institute of America	Personell Institute of America
8. Pritchard and Kayella	Pritchard and Kayella
9. D. C. Victor Elec.	A. C. Victor Elec.
10. Elfrein and Mattick	Elfrein and Mattrick
11. Hector's Bar-B-Q	Hector's Bar B-Q
12. Raymodna and Sharpe	Raymond and Sharpe
13. The Marquisea Company	The Marquisea Company
14. Thorp Noland and Son	Thorp Noland and Son
15. Parke Davis and Co.	Park Davis and Co.

(For scoring, see page 125.)

INFORMATIONAL RANGE TEST—No. 1

The following twenty words or names are connected with some particular field of knowledge or activity. Name the fields or activities. Allow 3 minutes.

1. Darwin
2. outriggers
3. Pavlova
4. Chippendale
5. a cappella
6. Titian
7. Ionic, Doric
8. Adam Smith
9. sisal
10. transformer
11. iconoscope
12. seismograph
13. Appian Way
14. cinchona tree
15. cracking process
16. Bessemer process
17. Zoroaster
18. conservation of energy
19. binomial theorem
20. Aesop

(For scoring, see page 125.)

INFORMATIONAL RANGE TEST—No. 2

The following twenty words or names are connected with some particular field of knowledge or activity. Name the fields or activities. Allow 3 minutes.

1. Rosetta Stone
2. gerund
3. philatelist
4. John Milton
5. Poseidon
6. Dead Sea scrolls
7. Genghis Khan
8. Plato
9. sourdough
10. Roald Amundsen
11. breeches bouy
12. cantilever
13. bronchoscope
14. caries
15. catamaran
16. Beethoven
17. Bertillon
18. ichthyology
19. marathon
20. marimba

(For scoring, see pages 125 and 126.)

INFORMATIONAL RANGE TEST—No. 3

The following twenty words or names are connected with some particular field of knowledge or activity. Name the fields or activities. Allow 3 minutes.

1. Braille
2. ohm
3. Zeus
4. deposition
5. Veda
6. tuning fork
7. osmosis
8. Copernicus
9. stethoscope
10. grand slammer
11. Plimsoll line
12. silo
13. coping saw
14. Marquis of Queensbury
15. sextant
16. actuary
17. Rhode Island Red
18. afterburner
19. Neanderthal
20. snorkel

(For scoring, see page 126.)

BUSINESS AND INDUSTRIAL INFORMATION TEST—No. 1

Our interests are often influenced by our aptitudes. A person with an aptitude for business and industry will usually build up considerable information on it from the reading he does, his natural experience, and his selective process of "remembering" what interests him.

Try this test of the range of your knowledge in this field: For each of the following statements list T (for true) or F (for false) on a separate sheet of paper.

Allow 2 minutes.

1. An alloy is a mixture of different metals by fusion.

2. Tungsten added to steel makes the steel more pliable and malleable.

3. Ad valorem means according to value, as a tax imposed on the shipping value of goods.

4. The slide rule is a multiplying device.

5. Amortization is the paying off of a debt in installments.

6. When a labor dispute is arbitrated, it must be litigated in the courts.

7. A balance sheet can only be made from a double entry bookkeeping system.

8. A Wall Street bear hopes that stock prices will rise sharply.

9. Carloadings are an important barometer of business conditions.

10. In a "closed shop," the employees may not belong to a union.

11. Commercial paper does not include bills of exchange.

12. A corporation may survive the death of its stockholders and officers.

(For scoring, see page 126.)

BUSINESS AND INDUSTRIAL
INFORMATION TEST—No. 2

Follow the same directions as for the preceding test.

1. Fiat money is paper money with no backing except decree of a government that it will be legal tender.

2. Gresham's Law is that bad money tends to drive good money out of circulation.

3. Jettisoning a cargo means selling it at the lowest bid.

4. The Old Lady of Threadneedle Street is a former British actress who sells violets.

5. A layout is a rough plan or outline, especially in the advertising field.

6. A promissory note must contain an unconditional promise to pay a certain sum of money.

7. Frederick W. Taylor was a pioneer in the field of scientific management.

8. A yellow dog contract is a contract of employment whereunder the employee agrees not to join a labor union.

9. Par value is a term used to represent the book value of a stock.

10. Prime cost is the initial cost of an article.

11. On consignment means that goods may be returned if not satisfactory.

12. Net profit is determined by finding the difference between manufacturing cost and the selling price.

(For scoring, see page 127.)

PERSONALITY TRAIT TEST—No. 1

Do you know what your dominant personality traits are? If you take the following 2 tests with care and thoughtfulness, you may gain new insight into your emotional make-up.

The tests consist of famous proverbs and familiar literary quotations, each followed by 4 or 5 possible interpretations. Choose from among those given the statement you think best interprets the proverb or quotation. Try to choose the answer which you should give—and have to defend—if you were discussing the proverb's or quotation's meaning with a group of friends.

Do not look up the answer to any one test until you have completed both tests.

PROVERB #1: "A rolling stone gathers no moss."

A. A person who never stays in one place or one job for very long will never attain success.

B. If you don't want to have moss grow on you, you have to keep active.

C. A man owes it to himself, his friends, and his family to do what life requires of him, and he should settle down.

D. What would a rolling stone want with moss, anyway?

E. In the long run, what effort a man puts into life in work pays off for him financially, socially, and personally. That's the way it is under our way of life.

PROVERB #2: "Don't cross your bridges until you get to them."

A. There's no point in worrying about troubles until they arise —though we should prepare for them.

B. Trust in the future and have faith in God.

C. Never mind tomorrow's problems—do a good job on today's.

D—You never know what's on the other side until you get up to the bridge, anyway.

PROVERB #3: "A stitch in time saves nine."

A. A person owes it to others to keep things in order—to keep his life tidy.

B. It pays to repair things before they fall apart.

C. Good housekeeping in our lives is a requirement for happiness.

D. Buy the best and you will have fewer worries.

PERSONALITY TRAIT TEST—No. 2

See instructions for previous test.

QUOTATION #1: A Book of Verses underneath the Bough,
    A Jug of Wine, a Loaf of Bread—and Thou
        Beside me singing in the Wilderness—
    Oh, Wilderness were Paradise enow!
        —*Omar Khayyam* (The Rubaiyat)

A. Happiness is where we find it.

B. If you make up your mind to it, you can assure finding happiness for yourself.

C. Happiness is right around us if we take a close enough look.

D. The author is trying to tell us we would be wise to accept the simple things and find enjoyment in them . . . that we'll be happy as a result, and that's what we really want.

E. The author apparently thinks that happiness and contentment in life can be found without much planning.

QUOTATION #2: There is a tide in the affairs of men,
    Which, taken at the flood, leads on to fortune;
        Omitted, all the voyage of their life
    Is bound in shallows and in miseries.
        —*Shakespeare* (Julius Caesar)

A. I'd better be on the watch when opportunity knocks or I'll miss an important chance to go places.

86

B. The pattern of life is such that it pays to watch what you do or you can wind up behind the 8-ball.

C. When you get your chance, make the most of it.

D. The person who plans his life well will make out all right under the laws of nature.

E. In many cases where people fail in life, it can be traced to circumstances and events over which they had little control.

QUOTATION #3: "No man is an island, entire of itself."
                                        —*John Donne*

A. To get where I want to go in life, I must realize I need the help of others.

B. We must all consider the needs and the wants of each other.

C. I am the captain of my soul, true enough, but I must make my way in life with many other captains.

D. The man who acts without regard for others fails to take into account that he is a social animal.

E. In planning your life, the inevitable influence which others will exert upon you should be taken into full account.

(For scoring, see pages 127 and 128.)

SCORING SECTION

WORD MEMORY TESTS

There are 64 possible points in each test. For each omitted word deduct 2 points. For each word out of original order, deduct 1 point.

54 or better   Excellent
48 to 54   Good
40 to 48   Fair
Less   You can improve your memory with practice

AUDITORY MEMORY TEST

The passage contained 12 essential points or ideas:

sailor	beware wild animals
shipwrecked	find food
reaches shore alone	beware poisonous things
wild country	look for people
find water	get a fire ready
find shelter	to attract ships

11 or 12   Excellent
9 or 10   Good
7 or 8   Fair
Less   Concentrate more as you read

MAP MEMORY TEST—No. 1

Compare your map with the original on page 10. There are 13 designations on the map. For each one you omitted, count 1 demerit.

For any perimeter line or street line you omitted, count 1 demerit.

For any designation you mislabeled, count 2 demerits.

Up to 2 demerits	Excellent map memory
3 to 5 demerits	Good
6 demerits	Fair
7 or more	Poor

MAP MEMORY TEST—No. 2

Compare your map with the original on page 11. There are 14 countries on the map. For each country you omitted, count 1 demerit.

For each country you included on the map but misnamed, count 2 demerits.

For a badly jumbled map, count 9 demerits.

Up to 4 demerits	Excellent
5 to 7 demerits	Good
8 demerits	Fair
9 or more	Poor

VISUAL AND AUDITORY MEMORY TEST

The passage used contained 12 essential points or ideas:

strange railroad station
in the Orient
trains arrive from north and
   south
often late
large waiting room, second floor
people sleep there

English is spoken
but no Englishmen there
built in 1912
mixed architecture
walls blackened by smoke
never cleaned

Scoring is the same as for the previous test.

VISUAL DESIGN TEST—No. 1

If top and bottom lines are symmetrical and parallel.... 2 credits
If your drawing follows the same design, a spread-formed Letter M .... 2 credits
If you placed the 2 small circles correctly .... 2 credits
If you had the 2 small circles but placed them incorrectly .... 1 credit
If you used double lines in making the form of the letter M .... 2 credits
If you placed the 2 long dashes correctly .... 2 credits
If you have the 2 dashes but placed incorrectly .... 1 credit

10 credits	Excellent
9 credits	Good
8 credits	Fair
Less	Your memory needs training, and even if you're not artistically inclined, you can aim for neatness

VISUAL DESIGN TEST—No. 2

For carefully drawn oblong .... 1 credit
For circle symmetrically placed within oblong .... 1 credit
For symmetrically drawn square within the circle, four
corners *touching* the circle .... 2 credits
For crisscross lines within the square .... 1 credit
For straight line bisecting the square and touching
the circle top and bottom .... 2 credits

7 credits	Excellent
6 credits	Good
5 credits	Fair
Less	Poor

ARTISTIC PERCEPTION TEST

1. mouth
2. eye
3. nose
4. spoon in right hand
5. chimney through roof (no credit for smoke)
6. ear
7. filament wires
8. stamp
9. strings
10. rivet at other end of knife
11. trigger
12. tail
13. leg on left side (not a claw)
14. one cat's shadow
15. a bowling ball for the man, placed in his hand
16. net
17. left arm
18. knob on television set
19. hand and powder puff in mirror
20. diamond in upper left of card

16-20 right	Excellent
14 or 15 right	Good
12 or 13 right	Fair
Less	Poor

VISUAL MEMORY TEST—No. 1

Some—but not all—of the forms you studied on page 14 are repeated among the forms below. On a separate sheet of paper list by number those you think are repeated, then confirm your selection by consulting page 14 again and score yourself.

0 or 1 mistake	Excellent visual memory
2 or 3	Good
4	Fair
5 or more	Poor

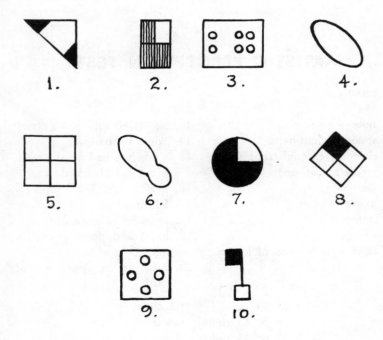

VISUAL MEMORY TEST—No. 2

Some of the forms you studied on page 15 are repeated among the forms below. On a separate sheet of paper list by number those you think are repeated. Then confirm your selections by consulting page 15 again and score yourself according to the previous test.

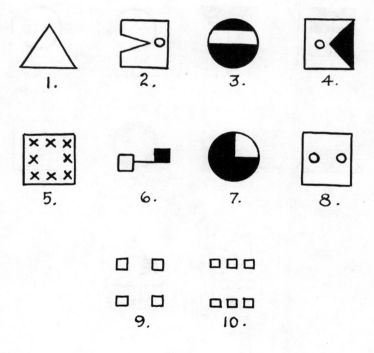

VISUAL MEMORY TEST—No. 3

Some of the forms you studied on page 16 are repeated among the forms below. On a separate sheet of paper list by number those you think are repeated. Then confirm your selections by consulting page 16 again and score yourself according to the previous tests.

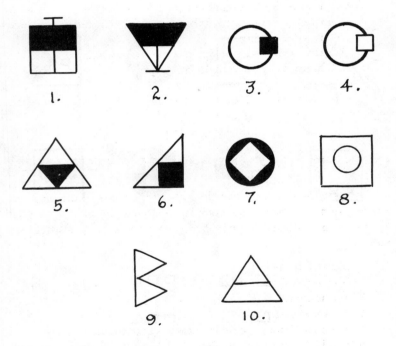

NAME MEMORY TEST

On a separate sheet of paper write down the answers to the following questions. There is no time limit. When you have answered as completely as possible, turn to page 17 to check your answers (15 items in all) and score your ability to remember names according to the scoring below.

1. What was the last name of the foreman?
2. What were the last names of his two workers?
3. Name the fraternal order they belonged to.
4. When did this meeting take place?
5. What was the first name of the foreman?
6. What were the first names of the two workers?
7. Two flags were carried. What were their background colors?
8. What did each flag say?
9. What was the color of the lettering on each flag?
10. When would election night be?

12 to 15	Excellent
10 or 11	Good
Less	Fair

OBSERVATION AND MEMORY TEST—No. 1

Answer the following questions about the scene of the accident. Allow 4 minutes, then check your answers with the picture on page 20 and allow yourself 1 point for each answer that is essentially correct.

1. What was the date?
2. The approximate time?
3. Bus number?
4. Was taxi occupied?
5. Describe damage to taxi: extent, where situated.
6. Could bus damage be described from your vantage point?
7. Did bus driver appear injured?
8. Describe apparent injuries to taxi driver.

9. Name on the ambulance?
10. In which direction was the taxi going?
11. In which direction was the bus going?
12. Describe the apparent point of impact.
13. Which vehicle struck the other?
14. What local news event was posted?
15. Name the newspaper building in the scene.
16. What was the destination of the bus?
17. Describe the vehicle stopped behind the taxi.
18. Name the two streets at the intersection.
19. Give the taxi's license number.
20. Give the bus's license number.

15 to 20	Good
12 to 14	Fair
Less	Poor

OBSERVATION AND MEMORY TEST—No. 2

Score 1 point for each correct item. Deduct 1 point for any item you included which is not actually in the scene. The picture contains the following 30 items:

boy	clock	vase
girl	mantel	barometer
kitten	small table	lamp
dog	large table	book
tricycle	rug	drapes
doll	picture	curtains
piano	birdcage	radiator
mirror	door	ashtray
window	television set	shade
fireplace	flowers	electric outlet

25 or more	Excellent		18 to 20	Fair
21 to 24	Good		Less	Poor

REASONING TEST—No. 1

1. 20.
2. 12.
3. The early bird catches the worm.
4. 2 5   3 6   5 8   1 4   6 9.
5. The sun, since the earth revolves around the sun.
6. 40 inches (reduced by one-ninth).
7. 3.
8. 8 feet.

7 or 8 correct	Excellent
6	Good
5	Satisfactory
Less	Poor

REASONING TEST—No. 2

1. Change 65 to 64, since the series is being raised by multiplying each number by 2.

2. Change 15 to 16, since the series is the successive squares of 2.

3. 30.

4. (c).

5. (c).

6. (c).

7. (b).

8. "While the cat's away, the mice will play."

Scoring is the same as for previous test.

REASONING TEST—No. 3

1. (c).
2. (d).
3. (a).

4. First line calls for 2 and 1.
   Next line calls for 1 and ⅓.

5. It is usually very *difficult* to become *acquainted* with people who are *very* timid. (Note: Any similar words, such as *excessively* in place of *very*, are acceptable if they make the same general sense.)

6. A reasonable *amount* of sleep is usually *required* if a person is to *maintain* a high *degree* of efficiency (see note above).

7. 6 hours (3 hours at 20 m.p.h. and 3 hours at 30 m.p.h.).

8. (d).

Scoring is the same as for the previous tests.

WORD RELATIONSHIP TEST—No. 1

The following words have the least association with the word groupings of the test. If you're in doubt about them, consult the dictionary. Vocabulary as well as general knowledge was involved in this test.

1.	grapefruit	(not a meal)
2.	tiger	(not domestic)
3.	letter	(not printed)
4.	recline	(the least in degree toward slumber)
5.	tree	(a single thing)
6.	hen	(other three are more closely related)
7.	Albany	(not a state)
8.	whimper	(a subdued sound)
9.	stockings	(not in the shoe family)
10.	picture	(smallest, most limited in size)
11.	Sun	(not a planet)
12.	dawn	(the others are P.M.)

12 correct	Excellent
10 or 11	Good
8 or 9	Fair
Under 8	Poor

WORD RELATIONSHIP TEST—No. 2

The following words have the least association with the word groupings of the test:

1.	atoll	(the others are wet grounds)
2.	current	(the others are necessarily wind manifestations)
3.	grudging	(unwilling)
4.	sprung	(a defect)
5.	curare	(a poison)
6.	water	(not an element)
7.	Tauri	(a constellation, not a single star)
8.	civet	(a carnivorous cat, not cattle)
9.	ulna	(a bone, not a muscle of the body)
10.	pelvis	(not a bone of the leg)
11.	Darwin	(not a religious leader)
12.	parishioner	(not of the priesthood)

10 or more	Excellent
8 or 9	Good
6 or 7	Fair
Less	Try to improve your word power

CAUSE AND EFFECT TEST

The following words are most readily associated as the effect of the cause words used in this test. However, if you selected a word that you believe is equally good, check its use with the dictionary.

For each of the following words, or any equally good word, allow yourself 2 points. If the word you selected has some relationship but is not as good a choice as the word we provide (determine this from the dictionary), allow 1 point. If you chose a word that isn't an effect word, you don't score for it.

1. nourishment .... strength
2. melting snows .... floods
3. hunger .... starvation
4. dirt .... disease
5. exercise ...... sweat or fatigue
6. effort .... achievement
7. cold .... ice, discomfort
8. injury .... pain, shock
9. crime .... punishment
10. work .... pay, wages
11. practice .... skill
12. beauty .... admiration
13. debt .... troubles
14. piano .... music

24 or more	Excellent
20 to 23	Good
16 to 20	Fair
Less	Poor

POWER TO INTERPRET TEST

1. (j) and (l)
2. (f) and (k)
3. (b) and (h)
4. (e) and (g)
5. (c) and (i)
6. (d) and (m)
7. (a) and (n)

13 or 14 right	Excellent
11 or 12	Good
10	Fair
Less	Insufficient grasp of what you read

NUMBER RELATIONSHIP TEST—No. 1

A. 31 (Rule: add 2, deduct 2; add 3, deduct 3; add 4, etc.)
B. 1 (Rule: repeat twice, deduct 2; repeat twice, deduct 2)
C. 7 (Rule: add 2, add 2, add 2; then deduct 2, deduct 2, etc.)
D. 27 (Rule: multiply by 3, divide by 2, multiply by 1; repeat)
E. 18 (Rule: add 1, deduct 2, add 3, deduct 4, etc.)
F. 39 (Rule: add 3, add 6, add 9, etc.)

All correct	Excellent
5 right	Good

4 right   Fair
Less   Poor mathematical comprehension

NUMBER RELATIONSHIP TEST—No. 2

A. 1 (Rule: add 1, add 1, deduct 2; repeat)
B. 20 (Rule: divide by 2, add 5; repeat)
C. 40 (Rule: add 3 each time)
D. 8 (Rule: divide by 2, add 4; repeat)
E. 38 (Rule: multiply by 2, subtract 3; repeat)
F. 2 (Rule: deduct 3, divide by 2; deduct 4, divide by 2; deduct 5, divide by 2, etc.)

NUMBER RELATIONSHIP TEST—No. 3

A. 17 (Rule: add 3, divide by 3, multiply by 2; repeat)
B. 0 (Rule: deduct 4, add 2, divide by 3; repeat)
C. 10 (Rule: add 3, deduct 1, add zero; repeat)
D. 22 (Rule: add 1, add 3, add 6; repeat)
E. 19 (Rule: add 2, deduct 3, add 4, deduct 5, etc.)
F. 15 (Rule: add 1, deduct 2, multiply by 3, divide by 4; repeat)
Scoring is the same as for the previous tests.

NUMBER RELATIONSHIP TEST—No. 4

A. 3 (Rule: divide by 2, deduct 2; repeat)
B. 8 (Rule: divide by 3, multiply by 2; repeat)
C. 34 (Rule: deduct 8's)
D. 20 (Rule: deduct 1, add 2; deduct 2, add 3; deduct 3, add 4, etc.
E. 12 (Rule: add 3, deduct 2; repeat)
F. 14 (Rule: add 2, add 2, deduct 2; repeat)
Scoring is the same as for the 3 previous tests.

WORD RELATIONSHIP AND GENERAL KNOWLEDGE TEST—No. 1

1. Sugar is gotten from sea water. *False.*

2. At times, every person makes mistakes. *True.*

3. The barber's razor once rated as a medical tool. *True.*

4. The barometer is a device for measuring the pressure of the atmosphere. *True.*

5. Belleau Woods was where the Germans stopped the U. S. Marines in World War I. *False.* or: Belleau Woods was where the U. S. Marines stopped the Germans in World War I. *True.*

6. Wheat is one of the minor crops of Soviet Russia. *False.*

7. The Champs Elysees is one of the main avenues of Marseille. *False.*

8. The Channel Islands are a group of islands in the English Channel. *True.*

9. The cirrus cloud is a detached cloud of delicate appearance. *True.*

10. Among the animals, the cheetah can attain a speed of 100 miles per hour. *False.*

11. To primitive people living on a small island, the world seems a small place. *True.*

12. Tea is chiefly grown in hilly countries of southern and eastern Asia. *True.*

10 or more wholly correct	Excellent
9	Good
8	Fair
Less	Poor

WORD RELATIONSHIP AND GENERAL KNOWLEDGE TEST—No. 2

1. Aluminum is the lightest metal in common use. *True.*

2. In the Fahrenheit scale, the boiling point of water is 100 degrees. *False.*

3. Except for hydrogen, helium is the lightest gas. *True.* or: Except for helium, hydrogen is the lightest gas. *False.*

4. The relation of bacteria to disease was established by Louis Pasteur. *True.*

5. The bighorn is a species of buffalo found in western America. *False.*

6. The femur, tibia, and fibula are important bones of the human leg. *True.*

7. Kirk Douglas played the part of Vincent van Gogh in the movies. *True.*

8. The first successful railroad locomotive was built by Robert Fulton. *False.*

9. Coal tar is an oily black pitch distilled from bituminous coal. *True.*

10. To one living at the north pole, the pole star would always be directly overhead. *True.*

11. Acids are compounds containing hydrogen and a non-metallic element. *True.*

12. The Jacobins were an unimportant political party during the French revolution. *False.*

Scoring is the same as previous test.

MATHEMATICAL JUDGMENT TEST—No. 1

1. $30,000. 2. 30. 3. $3.25. 4. $.40. 5. 28.

All 5 correct	Excellent
4	Good
Less	Poor mathematical judgment

MATHEMATICAL JUDGMENT TEST—No. 2

1. $90. 2. $400. 3. 36 hours, 15 minutes. 4. 8.2%. 5. Problem (b).

Scoring is the same as previous test.

MATHEMATICAL JUDGMENT TEST—No. 3

1. 1000. 2. 160. 3. 1½. 4. 6. 5. 12.

Scoring is the same as previous test.

MECHANICAL COMPREHENSION TEST No. 1

1. A, transmitting its energy to B, will tend to come to rest.
2. The greater absorption of the radiant energy of the sunlight by the black jacket will cause the snow under it to melt faster.
3. The far smaller square footage of parachute B will cause it to descend faster, despite the lighter weight.
4. Shaft B will turn faster.
5. Gear C will move in direction B.

Scoring: anything less than 4 right shows poor mechanical understanding.

MECHANICAL COMPREHENSION TEST
No. 2

1. Picture B, since water rises only to its own level.
2. Cord A will break, because it sustains the whole force pulling on B as well as the weight of M.
3. In direction A, to replace the hot air moving up.
4. Shears B because of the closer fulcrum.
5. From direction A (notice the way the casters point).

Scoring is the same as previous test.

MECHANICAL COMPREHENSION TEST
No. 3

1. 72 pounds.
2. Can B.
3. In direction B.
4. Since point O is the center of the mass, the triangle would remain in balance.
5. Water would rise (because of expansion of the air).

MECHANICAL COMPREHENSION TEST
No. 4

1. Bottle A is the colder
2. The ball will move in direction C
3. Gear C
4. The job is easier for B
5. Windlass A

TOOL COMPREHENSION TEST—No. 1

1. and 5. (Hose nozzle and pump)
2. and 8. (Hydrometer and battery)
4. and 6. (Cams)
3. and 7. (Lock parts)

You must get all 4 pairs correct to show any significant degree of tool comprehension.

TOOL COMPREHENSION TEST—No. 2

1. and 7. (Grinder and knife blade)
2. and 6. (Anvil and hammer)
3. and 5. (Saw and mitre box)
4. and 8. (Plane and vise)

Scoring is the same as previous test.

WORD POWER TEST—No. 1

1. Usury
2. Abdication
3. Harmony
4. Omelet
5. Ravenous
6. Hobby

6 correct	Excellent
5 correct	Good
4 correct	Fair
Less	Poor word power

WORD POWER TEST—No. 2

1. Mermaid
2. Eternity or Infinity
3. Hermit
4. Talon
5. Refrigerator
6. Salary

Scoring is the same as previous test.

WORD POWER TEST—No. 3

1. Vacuum
2. Irrigation
3. Silhouette
4. Hydrogen
5. Hedonism
6. Insomnia

Scoring is the same as previous tests.

WORD MEANING TEST—No. 1

1. Gradual .... sudden (opposite)
2. Vapid .... insipid (same)
3. Seemly .... fit (same)
4. Devout .... impious (opposite)
5. Contemptible .... despicable (same)
6. Energetic .... apathetic (opposite)
7. Gaunt .... haggard (same)
8. Eternal .... temporary (opposite)

7 or 8 correct	Excellent
6	Good
Less	Poor vocabulary power

WORD MEANING TEST—No. 2

1. Envious .... covetous (same)
2. Reserved .... reticent (same)
3. Identical .... heterogeneous (opposite)
4. Moderate .... extreme (opposite)
5. Romantic .... prosaic (opposite)
6. Liberal .... generous (same)
7. Round .... circular (same)
8. Cruel .... vicious (same)

Scoring is the same as previous test.

WORD RELATIONSHIP TEST—No. 3

1. suitcase
2. see
3. statue
4. cars

5. climax
6. quantity
7. cows
8. prediction

7 or 8 correct	Excellent
6	Good
Less	Poor word power

WORD RELATIONSHIP TEST—No. 4

1. rose
2. duet
3. caution
4. orchestra

5. suffocation
6. time
7. originate
8. knee

Scoring is the same as previous test.

SPEED OF IMAGINATION TEST—No. 1

This was a test of your speed in thinking and in imagination. We can't possibly cover all the important changes on this page, so you will have to grade yourself to some degree. How many answers did you list? Be very honest in reviewing your answers and satisfy yourself that they are truly applicable and important. Here are some illustrative answers:

Paralyze business
Paralyze railroads
Paralyze shipping
Decrease output of products
Increase government regulation
Produce emergency in heating
Speed up inventions and chemical research

Deplete forests
Change many occupations
Bankrupt many companies
Food emergencies
Profiteering
Crime wave
Warmer clothing needed
Big increase in water power use, etc.

10 or more	Excellent
8 or 9	Good
6 or 7	Fair
Under 6	Poor

SPEED OF IMAGINATION TEST—No. 2

As with Speed of Imagination Test—No. 1, we can't give you all the possible answers. Be honest and critical with yourself in reviewing your answers. Satisfy yourself that they are applicable and important. Here are some illustrations:

Disrupt medical service
Create near panic
Require government intervention
Cause religious upheaval
Impair essential services
Restrict travel severely
Create labor shortage
Ruin insurance companies
Divert funds to medical research
Impoverish families
Alter society

Scoring is the same as previous test.

CONSTRUCTIVE IMAGINATION TESTS
Nos. 1 and 2

Count the practical ideas you listed. Never mind the actual value of the ideas unless, as you reflect on them, they seem patently absurd. The object of these tests is to measure your ability to apply past experience to a new situation.

25 or more	Excellent
20 to 24	Good
16 to 19	Fair
Less	You need to exercise your imagination more

No. 3

The following words can be formed from the given letters:

a, air, airy, arise, art, arty, as, at, aye, ear, east, easy, eat, I, irate, ire, is, it, its, oar, oat, or, ore, oyster, raise, rat, rate, ratio, ray, reasty, rest, ret, rise, rite, roast, rose, rot, rote, rye, sat, sate, say, sear, seat, sir, sire, sit, site, soar, sore, sort, sot, soy, star, stare, stay, stir, store, story, stray, tar, tare, tear, to, toe, tory, toy, tray, trey, year, yeast, yes, yore.

35 or more words	Exceptional
30 to 35	Excellent
25 to 30	Good
20 to 25	Fair
Less	You need more practice

No. 4

The following words can be formed from the given letters:

a, ail, air, ale, alp, ape, are, ear, earl, era, I, ire, rail, rale, rap, rape, real, reap, rial, rile, rip, ripe, lair, lap, lea, leap, lei, liar, lie, lira, lip, pa, pail, pair, pal, pale, paler, par, pare, pea, peal, pear, pearl, per, peril, peri, pi, pie, pier, pile, plea, and plier.

40 or better	Excellent
35 to 40	Good
30 to 35	Fair
Under 30	Keep trying!

CREATIVE IMAGINATION TEST—No. 1

You should have accepted all ten suggested uses for the empty bottle. Everything listed is within the realm of possible use for it—even the musical instrument itemization, since several bottles can be filled with water to varying degrees and made to respond to a recognizable scale.

Failure on your part to see some degree of usefulness for the bottle in all ten listed ways indicates that conventional patterns of thought have a restrictive influence on your creative processes. If you ruled out three or more of the listed uses, you should give your imagination greater scope.

CREATIVE IMAGINATION TEST—No. 2

We won't try to give a complete list of the possible unconventional (but practical) uses of the items set forth. The following list is simply illustrative. The creative imagination test is this: you should have been able to think of at least one use for *all ten* of the items in the 3 minutes allowed. Judge yourself critically on the answers you came up with. If you had only seven or fewer reasonably correct answers, you are a victim of "functional fixation"—you are losing your originality and creativity in a general acceptance of things as they are. If you have 8 answers you're just Fair; 9, Good; only 10 can be considered Excellent.

1. hammer: to crack walnuts.
2. nail: as a fuse in an electrical circuit (BUT DON'T TRY IT!).
3. pencil: to separate small objects in a bowl.
4. hairpin: as an improvised cotter pin.
5. coin: to lift a jar cap.

6. newspaper: (rolled up) as a fly swatter.

7. lampshade: to create an improvised hat for fun at a party.

8. inkwell: as a paperweight.

9. circular doily: to make an improvised dartboard or arrow target.

10. straw handbag: to store small toys.

CREATIVE IMAGINATION TEST—No. 3

The following answers are merely illustrative of the type of answer you could give. Judge yourself critically on the answers you came up with. Throw out any which are wholly inapplicable. If you provided acceptable answers for all 10 objects, you have an excellent imaginative sense for perceiving *problems* that exist in a situation, or shortcomings therein. A score of 9 is Good; 8 is Fair; anything less shows lack of creative imagination.

1. food mixer: a splashboard rigged up as an umbrella shield above the mixing blades.

2. radio: a device that turns off automatically if the station goes off the air for more than two minutes.

3. washing machine: device that would set off an alarm if the detergent or soap used was too weak or too strong for the setting.

4. vacuum cleaner: vertical fan to cool the operator in hot weather.

5. toaster: thermostat to keep the bread warm for another two minutes after toasting process, if not immediately removed.

6. refrigerator: alarm device if the refrigerant leaks.

7. steam iron: frontal light to illuminate the goods being ironed.

8. floor polisher: mechanism to lift the brushes so shoes could be polished.

9. tv set: automatic dial to turn on the set at desired time.

10. electric alarm clock: warning device that would sound if the electricity cut off during the night.

CREATIVE IMAGINATION TEST—No. 4

A: Three men in a tub.
B: The owl and the pussy cat getting ready to set out to sea.
C: Humpty Dumpty in the act of taking his great fall.
D: Little Bo Peep's sheep coming home, dragging their tails behind them.

All 4 correct, Excellent. Anything less, Unsatisfactory (unless your childhood didn't include a familiarity with the nursery rhymes and tales)

CREATIVE IMAGINATION TEST—No. 5

Figure A: Dog (or cat) entering a door.
B: Ocean as seen from a porthole.
C: Three blind mice.
D: Small garage; long car.

All 4 correct, Excellent. (Anything less, relax your imagination.)

CONCENTRATION TEST—No. 1

There were 24 pairs of numbers to be circled:

a.	(9 1)	(2 8)	(3 7)	Total	3
b.	(6 4)	(8 2)			2
c.	(3 7)	(2 8)			2
d.	(5 5)	(2 8)	(7 3)	(9 1)	4
e.	(2 8)	(3 7)			2
f.	(3 7)				1
g.	(3 7)	(8 2)	(4 6)	(5 5)	4
h.	(8 2)	(3 7)	(4 6)		3
i.	(5 5)	(9 1)			2
j.	(1 9)				1

20 or more	Excellent
18 or 19	Good
16 or 17	Fair
Less	Poor concentrative power

CONCENTRATION TEST—No. 2

93 — 86 — 79 — 72 — 65 — 58 — 51
44 — 37 — 30 — 23 — 16 — 9 — 2

CONCENTRATION TEST—No. 3

49 — 47 — 46 — 44 — 43 — 41 — 40 — 38 — 37 — 35 — 34 — 32
31 — 29 — 28 — 26 — 25 — 23 — 22 — 20 — 19 — 17 — 16 — 14
13 — 11 — 10 — 8 — 7 — 5 — 4 — 2 — 1

CONCENTRATION TEST—No. 4

1. IF YOU
2. DO WELL THE
3. MINOR TASKS
4. WHICH YOU
5. ARE CALLED
6. UPON
7. TO PERFORM YOU
8. WILL HAVE BUT LITTLE
9. DIFFICULTY WITH
10. THE BIGGER ONES

20 or more	Excellent
18 or 19	Good
16 or 17	Fair
Less	Try harder to disregard extraneous disturbances

ACCURACY TEST—No. 1

The following pairs are the correct answers (the same):

1, 3, 4, 6, 10, 11, 13, 16, 17, 18, 20, 24, 25

For unfinished numbers count ½. For errors count 1 point.

Debit of 0 to 3	Excellent
Debit of 4 to 6	Good
Debit of 7 or 8	Fair
Debit over 8	Too careless

ACCURACY TEST—No. 2

The following pairs are the correct answers (the same):

1, 4, 7, 8, 9, 12, 16, 18, 19, 20, 23, 24

Scoring is the same as previous test.

THOROUGHNESS TEST—No. 1

1. 1 and 16
2. 5 and 7 and 18
3. 9
4. 3 and 19

5. 2 and 20
6. 8
7. 10

For each *exactly* correct answer allow yourself a credit of 2 points. Take no other credits.

12 or more credits	Excellent
10 or 11 credits	Good
9	Fair
Less	You worked either too quickly or too carelessly

THOROUGHNESS TEST—No. 2

1. 15
2. 4 and 17
3. 14 and 21
4. 6 and 13

5. 11
6. none
7. 12

Scoring is the same as the previous test.

ORGANIZING ABILITY TEST—No. 1

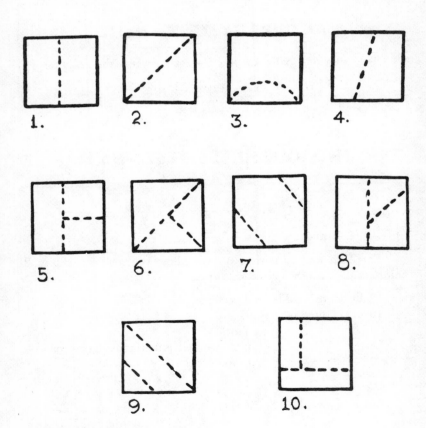

8 to 10 correct	Excellent
6 or 7 correct	Good
5 correct	Fair
Less	Poor

ORGANIZING ABILITY TEST—No. 2

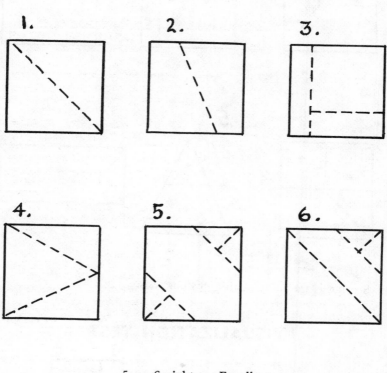

5 or 6 right	Excellent
4 right	Good
3 right	Fair
Less	Poor

Scoring is the same as the previous test.

ORGANIZING ABILITY TEST—No. 3

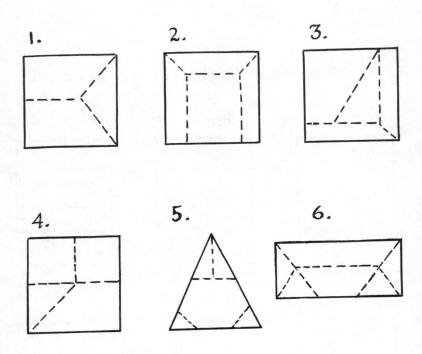

Scoring is the same as the previous test.

VISUALIZATION TEST

(a)	27	(g)	10
(b)	15	(h)	22
(c)	15	(i)	13
(d)	18	(j)	20
(e)	19	(k)	50
(f)	40		

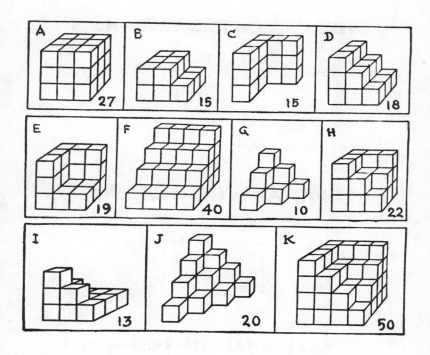

10 or 11 piles correctly figured	Excellent
8 or 9	Good
7	Fair
Less	Poor

SCORING FOR VISUAL ANALYSIS TESTS 1 THROUGH 5

5 correct	Excellent
4	Good
Less	You need to analyze your problems more carefully

VISUAL ANALYSIS TEST—No. 1

Line 1. Figure 2
Line 2. Figure 2
Line 3. Figure 5
Line 4. Figure 4
Line 5. Figure 1

(For scoring, see previous page.)

VISUAL ANALYSIS TEST—No. 2

Line 1. Figure 3
Line 2. Figure 5
Line 3. Figure 1
Line 4. Figure 2
Line 5. Figure 4

VISUAL ANALYSIS TEST—No. 3

Line 1. Figure 4
Line 2. Figure 4
Line 3. Figure 4
Line 4. Figure 2
Line 5. Figure 2

VISUAL ANALYSIS TEST—No. 4

Line 1. Figure 4
Line 2. Figure 3
Line 3. Figure 3
Line 4. Figure 3
Line 5. Figure 1

VISUAL ANALYSIS TEST—No. 5

Line 1.   Figure 5
Line 2.   Figure 3
Line 3.   Figure 4
Line 4.   Figure 4
Line 5.   Figure 5

PATTERN VISUALIZATION TESTS

Test—No. 1   1 and 3
Test—No. 2   2 (only)
Test—No. 3   1 (only)
Test—No. 4   1 and 2
Test—No. 5   3 (only)
Test—No. 6   1, 4 and 5
Test—No. 7   1 and 2
Test—No. 8   2 and 3

On the overall test of 8 pattern figures with 14 possible correct figures, credit yourself with 2 points for each correct figure picked but debit yourself with 1 point for each incorrect figure picked.

20 or better   Excellent
16 to 19   Good
12 to 15   Fair
Lower   Not everyone can visualize this way!

SPACE PERCEPTION TEST

The following answers are considered correct for the questions used. (This was not a test of knowledge, but of space measurement.)

1. 52 to 62 inches
2. 124 (ᔭ ≗ ʇ)
3. 9 o'clock
4. 4
5. 4

6. 18 to 22 inches
7. 10 to 12 inches
8. 1:15
9. 14 to 16 inches
10. "&" ("⅙")

9 or 10	Excellent
8	Good
7	Fair
Less	Poor

PRECISION TEST—No. 1

1 5 4 2 7 6 3 5 7 2 8 5 4 6 3 7 2 8 1 9 5 8 4 7 3
∸∪∟ N ∧ O ⊐ ∪ ∧ И X ∪ ∟ O ⊐ ∧ И X ∸ ⹀ ∪ X ∟ ∧ ⊐

6 2 5 1 9 2 8 3 7 4 6 5 9 4 8 3 7 2 6 1 5 4 6 3 7
O И ∪ ∸ ⹀ И X ⊐ ∧ ∟ O ∪ ⹀ ∟ X ⊐ ∧ И O ∸ ∪ ∟ O ⊐ ∧

45 to 50	Excellent
40 to 45	Good
35 to 40	Satisfactory
Less	You need to concentrate more on detail work

PRECISION TEST—No. 2

3 1 2 1 3 2 1 4 2 3 5 2 9 1 4
⊐ ∸ И ∸ ⊐ И ∸ ∟ И ⊐ ∪ И ⹀ ∸ ∟

6 3 1 5 4 2 7 6 3 8 7 2 9 5 4
O ⊐ ∸ ∪ ∟ И ∧ O ⊐ X ∧ И ⹀ ∪ ∟

6 3 7 2 8 1 9 5 8 4 7 3 6 9 5
O ⊐ ∧ И X ∸ ⹀ ∪ X ∟ ∧ ⊐ O ⹀ ∪

You score yourself on the number of seconds it took you, but you must add 2 seconds for each incorrect symbol.

Under 90 seconds	Excellent
90 to 100 seconds	Good
100 to 120 seconds	Fair
120 or more	You need to concentrate more on detail work

PRECISION TEST—No. 3

1	9	2	8	3	7	4	6	5	9	4	8	5	7	6
–	≈	И	X	Ⅎ	∧	∟	○	∪	≈	∟	X	∪	∧	○

9	3	8	6	4	1	5	7	2	6	2	4	8	1	3
≈	Ⅎ	X	○	∟	–	∪	∧	И	○	И	∟	X	–	Ⅎ

4	9	5	1	7	5	2	6	9	3	7	8	4	1	8
∟	≈	∪	–	∧	∪	И	○	≈	Ⅎ	∧	X	∟	–	X

Scoring is the same as the previous test.

MANUAL DEXTERITY TEST

Count 1 point for each tap correctly made. Deduct 2 points for each error. Count each of these as errors:

> a box you skipped
> two dots in same box
> dot striking a line

96 or more	Excellent
86 to 96	Good
80 to 84	Fair
Less	Poor

OFFICE MACHINE APTITUDE TEST—No. 1

1.	6	0	3	2	9.	4	0	1	5
2.	2	8	9	1	10.	0	3	6	1
3.	1	6	7	4	11.	1	7	1	6
4.	3	4	1	0	12.	1	2	3	1
5.	2	7	0	9	13.	5	2	3	5
6.	1	4	0	3	14.	6	9	3	5
7.	7	1	3	2	15.	4	1	4	9
8.	5	8	0	9					

If all 4 numbers are correct on a line, give yourself 1 credit. Deduct 1 credit from your total for any line containing one or more mistakes. Deduct ½ credit for each line not completed.

14 or more	Excellent
11 to 13	Good
8 to 10	Fair
Less	Poor

OFFICE MACHINE APTITUDE TEST—No. 2

1.	1	4	8	2	9.	3	6	9	1
2.	1	0	3	4	10.	7	4	5	6
3.	1	3	5	3	11.	4	2	6	7
4.	2	3	9	5	12.	6	3	0	4
5.	1	5	8	5	13.	8	2	3	7
6.	5	0	9	2	14.	5	9	3	0
7.	4	9	0	4	15.	7	2	4	3
8.	5	8	0	1					

Scoring is the same as the previous test.

COPYREADING APTITUDE TEST—No. 1

The following lines contain errors:

1   2   4   6   7   9   10   11   13   14

COPYREADING APTITUDE TEST—No. 2

The following lines contain errors:

1   2   3   4   6   7   9   10   11   12   15

Scoring for both tests: More than 3 errors in either test means that you are a careless copyreader. You can overcome this with practice.

INFORMATIONAL RANGE TEST—No. 1

1. biology
2. canoeing
3. dancing
4. furniture
5. singing
6. painting
7. architecture
8. economics
9. rope making
10. electricity
11. television
12. measuring earth tremors
13. road building
14. quinine (medicine)
15. gasoline production
16. steel industry
17. religion
18. physics
19. algebra
20. literature

16 or more	Excellent
14 or 15	Good
12 or 13	Fair
Less	Unsatisfactory (Start reading!)

INFORMATIONAL RANGE TEST—No. 2

1. archaeology or languages
2. grammar
3. stamp collecting
4. literature or poetry
5. mythology
6. religion
7. history
8. philosophy
9. gold mining
10. explorations
11. rescue work at sea
12. bridge building
13. medicine
14. dentistry

15. sailing, boating
16. music
17. fingerprinting
18. zoology (fish life)
19. racing
20. music (instruments)

16 or more	Excellent
14 or 15	Good
12 or 13	Fair
Less	Try a more varied reading diet

INFORMATIONAL RANGE TEST—No. 3

1. alphabet devised for the blind
2. electricity
3. mythology
4. law
5. religion (Hinduism)
6. musical instruments
7. botany, chemistry
8. astronomy
9. medicine
10. baseball
11. shipping
12. farming
13. carpentry
14. boxing, prizefighting
15. navigation, surveying
16. insurance
17. poultry raising
18. jet plane propulsion
19. anthropology
20. underwater operation

16 or more	Excellent
14 or 15	Good
12 or 13	Fair
Less	Unsatisfactory

BUSINESS AND INDUSTRIAL INFORMATION TEST—No. 1

1. True
2. False
3. True
4. True
5. True
6. False
7. True
8. False
9. True
10. False
11. False
12. True

11 or 12	Excellent
9 or 10	Good
7 or 8	Fair
Less	Your information range needs widening

BUSINESS AND INDUSTRIAL INFORMATION TEST—No. 2

1. True
2. True
3. False
4. False
5. True
6. True

7. True
8. True
9. False
10. False
11. False
12. False

Scoring is the same as the previous test.

PERSONALITY TRAIT TEST—No. 1

Don't expect the results of your selections on these tests to psychoanalyze you to a tee. They will merely give you an idea of your dominant traits and tendencies. Personalities are complex things, combining many overlapping traits. In these tests you were asked to choose the most appealing interpretations, but in making your choice you did not necessarily rule out other choices. You may only have relegated them to a less important place. However, if many of your choices lay in the same direction, you can see which way the wind blows!

Proverb 1. A—Practical and logical: you like to reason things out carefully

B—Irresponsible: you lack perseverance and seriousness

C—Moralistic: you tend to judge self and others firmly

D—Humorous: you are inclined to place sense of humor foremost

E—Conventional: you tend to conform and yield to authority

Proverb 2. A—Conventional
B—Moralistic
C—Practical and logical
D—Irresponsible

Proverb 3. A—Moralistic
B—Practical and logical
C—Conventional
D—Irresponsible

PERSONALITY TRAIT TEST—No. 2

Quotation 1. A—Practical
B—Foresighted: you tend to plan well
C—Moralistic
D—Conventional and moralistic
E—Irresponsible

Quotation 2. A—Self-interested: you tend to measure things in terms of personal outlook
B—Humorous and irresponsible
C—Practical and logical
D—Conventional
E—Moralistic

Quotation 3. A—Self-interested
B—Conventional
C—Moralistic
D—Objective: you tend to be humanitarian in view
E—Practical and logical

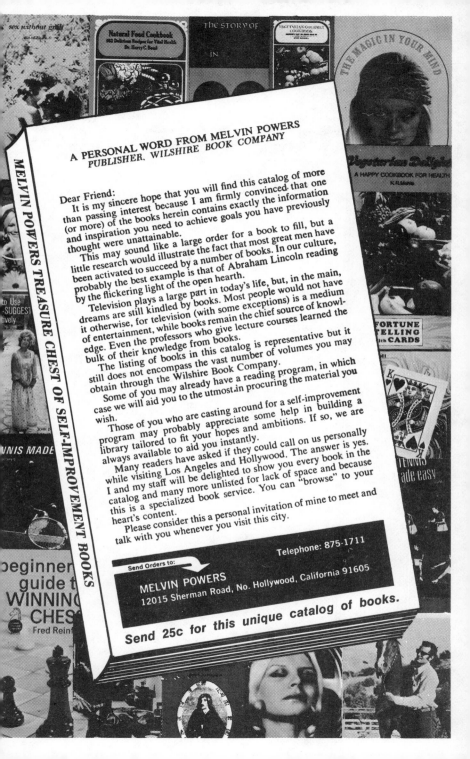

Melvin Powers
SELF-IMPROVEMENT
LIBRARY

ASTROLOGY

_____ASTROLOGY: A FASCINATING HISTORY *P. Naylor*	2.00
_____ASTROLOGY: HOW TO CHART YOUR HOROSCOPE *Max Heindel*	2.00
_____ASTROLOGY: YOUR PERSONAL SUN-SIGN GUIDE *Beatrice Ryder*	2.00
_____ASTROLOGY FOR EVERYDAY LIVING *Janet Harris*	2.00
_____ASTROLOGY MADE EASY *Astarte*	2.00
_____ASTROLOGY MADE PRACTICAL *Alexandra Kayhle*	2.00
_____ASTROLOGY, ROMANCE, YOU AND THE STARS *Anthony Norvell*	3.00
_____MY WORLD OF ASTROLOGY *Sydney Omarr*	3.00
_____THOUGHT DIAL *Sydney Omarr*	2.00
_____ZODIAC REVEALED *Rupert Gleadow*	2.00

BRIDGE & POKER

_____ADVANCED POKER STRATEGY & WINNING PLAY *A. D. Livingston*	2.00
_____BRIDGE BIDDING MADE EASY *Edwin Kantar*	5.00
_____BRIDGE CONVENTIONS *Edwin Kantar*	4.00
_____COMPLETE DEFENSIVE BRIDGE PLAY *Edwin B. Kantar*	10.00
_____HOW TO IMPROVE YOUR BRIDGE *Alfred Sheinwold*	2.00
_____HOW TO WIN AT POKER *Terence Reese & Anthony T. Watkins*	2.00
_____TEST YOUR BRIDGE PLAY *Edwin B. Kantar*	3.00

BUSINESS STUDY & REFERENCE

_____CONVERSATION MADE EASY *Elliot Russell*	2.00
_____EXAM SECRET *Dennis B. Jackson*	2.00
_____FIX-IT BOOK *Arthur Symons*	2.00
_____HOW TO BE A COMEDIAN FOR FUN & PROFIT *King & Laufer*	2.00
_____HOW TO DEVELOP A BETTER SPEAKING VOICE *M. Hellier*	2.00
_____HOW TO MAKE A FORTUNE IN REAL ESTATE *Albert Winnikoff*	3.00
_____HOW TO MAKE MONEY IN REAL ESTATE *Stanley L. McMichael*	2.00
_____INCREASE YOUR LEARNING POWER *Geoffrey A. Dudley*	2.00
_____MAGIC OF NUMBERS *Robert Tocquet*	2.00
_____PRACTICAL GUIDE TO BETTER CONCENTRATION *Melvin Powers*	2.00
_____PRACTICAL GUIDE TO PUBLIC SPEAKING *Maurice Forley*	2.00
_____7 DAYS TO FASTER READING *William S. Schaill*	2.00
_____SONGWRITERS' RHYMING DICTIONARY *Jane Shaw Whitfield*	3.00
_____SPELLING MADE EASY *Lester D. Basch & Dr. Milton Finkelstein*	2.00
_____STUDENT'S GUIDE TO BETTER GRADES *J. A. Rickard*	2.00
_____TEST YOURSELF — Find Your Hidden Talent *Jack Shafer*	2.00
_____YOUR WILL & WHAT TO DO ABOUT IT *Attorney Samuel G. Kling*	2.00

CHESS & CHECKERS

_____BEGINNER'S GUIDE TO WINNING CHESS *Fred Reinfeld*	2.00
_____BETTER CHESS — How to Play *Fred Reinfeld*	2.00
_____CHECKERS MADE EASY *Tom Wiswell*	2.00
_____CHESS IN TEN EASY LESSONS *Larry Evans*	2.00
_____CHESS MADE EASY *Milton L. Hanauer*	2.00
_____CHESS MASTERY — A New Approach *Fred Reinfeld*	2.00
_____CHESS PROBLEMS FOR BEGINNERS *edited by Fred Reinfeld*	2.00
_____CHESS SECRETS REVEALED *Fred Reinfeld*	2.00

Melvin Powers
SELF-IMPROVEMENT
LIBRARY

_____CHESS STRATEGY — An Expert's Guide _Fred Reinfeld_	2.00
_____CHESS TACTICS FOR BEGINNERS _edited by Fred Reinfeld_	2.00
_____CHESS THEORY & PRACTICE _Morry & Mitchell_	2.00
_____HOW TO WIN AT CHECKERS _Fred Reinfeld_	2.00
_____1001 BRILLIANT WAYS TO CHECKMATE _Fred Reinfeld_	2.00
_____1001 WINNING CHESS SACRIFICES & COMBINATIONS _Fred Reinfeld_	2.00

COOKERY & HERBS

_____CULPEPER'S HERBAL REMEDIES _Dr. Nicholas Culpeper_	2.00
_____FAST GOURMET COOKBOOK _Poppy Cannon_	2.50
_____HEALING POWER OF HERBS _May Bethel_	2.00
_____HERB HANDBOOK _Dawn MacLeod_	2.00
_____HERBS FOR COOKING AND HEALING _Dr. Donald Law_	2.00
_____HERBS FOR HEALTH How to Grow & Use Them _Louise Evans Doole_	2.00
_____HOME GARDEN COOKBOOK Delicious Natural Food Recipes _Ken Kraft_	3.00
_____NATURAL FOOD COOKBOOK _Dr. Harry C. Bond_	2.00
_____NATURE'S MEDICINES _Richard Lucas_	2.00
_____VEGETABLE GARDENING FOR BEGINNERS _Hugh Wiberg_	2.00
_____VEGETABLES FOR TODAY'S GARDENS _R. Milton Carleton_	2.00
_____VEGETARIAN COOKERY _Janet Walker_	2.00
_____VEGETARIAN COOKING MADE EASY & DELECTABLE _Veronica Vezza_	2.00
_____VEGETARIAN DELIGHTS — A Happy Cookbook for Health _K. R. Mehta_	2.00
_____VEGETARIAN GOURMET COOKBOOK _Joyce McKinnel_	2.00

HEALTH

_____DR. LINDNER'S SPECIAL WEIGHT CONTROL METHOD	1.00
_____GAYELORD HAUSER'S NEW GUIDE TO INTELLIGENT REDUCING	3.00
_____HELP YOURSELF TO BETTER SIGHT _Margaret Darst Corbett_	2.00
_____HOW TO IMPROVE YOUR VISION _Dr. Robert A. Kraskin_	2.00
_____HOW YOU CAN STOP SMOKING PERMANENTLY _Ernest Caldwell_	2.00
_____LSD — THE AGE OF MIND _Bernard Roseman_	2.00
_____MIND OVER PLATTER _Peter G. Lindner, M.D._	2.00
_____NEW CARBOHYDRATE DIET COUNTER _Patti Lopez-Pereira_	1.00
_____PSYCHEDELIC ECSTASY _William Marshall & Gilbert W. Taylor_	2.00
_____YOU CAN LEARN TO RELAX _Dr. Samuel Gutwirth_	2.00

HOBBIES

_____BLACKSTONE'S MODERN CARD TRICKS _Harry Blackstone_	2.00
_____BLACKSTONE'S SECRETS OF MAGIC _Harry Blackstone_	2.00
_____COIN COLLECTING FOR BEGINNERS _Burton Hobson & Fred Reinfeld_	2.00
_____400 FASCINATING MAGIC TRICKS YOU CAN DO _Howard Thurston_	3.00
_____GOULD'S GOLD & SILVER GUIDE TO COINS _Maurice Gould_	2.00
_____HOW I TURN JUNK INTO FUN AND PROFIT _Sari_	3.00
_____HOW TO WRITE A HIT SONG & SELL IT _Tommy Boyce_	7.00
_____JUGGLING MADE EASY _Rudolf Dittrich_	2.00
_____MAGIC MADE EASY _Byron Wels_	2.00
_____SEW SIMPLY, SEW RIGHT _Mini Rhea & F. Leighton_	2.00
_____STAMP COLLECTING FOR BEGINNERS _Burton Hobson_	2.00
_____STAMP COLLECTING FOR FUN & PROFIT _Frank Cetin_	2.00

Melvin Powers
SELF-IMPROVEMENT
LIBRARY

HORSE PLAYERS' WINNING GUIDES

BETTING HORSES TO WIN *Les Conklin*	2.00
HOW TO PICK WINNING HORSES *Bob McKnight*	2.00
HOW TO WIN AT THE RACES *Sam (The Genius) Lewin*	2.00
HOW YOU CAN BEAT THE RACES *Jack Kavanagh*	2.00
MAKING MONEY AT THE RACES *David Barr*	2.00
PAYDAY AT THE RACES *Les Conklin*	2.00
SMART HANDICAPPING MADE EASY *William Bauman*	2.00

HYPNOTISM

ADVANCED TECHNIQUES OF HYPNOSIS *Melvin Powers*	1.00
CHILDBIRTH WITH HYPNOSIS *William S. Kroger, M.D.*	2.00
HOW TO SOLVE YOUR SEX PROBLEMS WITH SELF-HYPNOSIS *Frank S. Caprio, M.D.*	2.00
HOW TO STOP SMOKING THRU SELF-HYPNOSIS *Leslie M. LeCron*	2.00
HOW TO USE AUTO-SUGGESTION EFFECTIVELY *John Duckworth*	2.00
HOW YOU CAN BOWL BETTER USING SELF-HYPNOSIS *Jack Heise*	2.00
HOW YOU CAN PLAY BETTER GOLF USING SELF-HYPNOSIS *Heise*	2.00
HYPNOSIS AND SELF-HYPNOSIS *Bernard Hollander, M.D.*	2.00
HYPNOTISM *(Originally published in 1893) Carl Sextus*	3.00
HYPNOTISM & PSYCHIC PHENOMENA *Simeon Edmunds*	2.00
HYPNOTISM MADE EASY *Dr. Ralph Winn*	2.00
HYPNOTISM MADE PRACTICAL *Louis Orton*	2.00
HYPNOTISM REVEALED *Melvin Powers*	1.00
HYPNOTISM TODAY *Leslie LeCron & Jean Bordeaux, Ph.D.*	2.00
MEDICAL HYPNOSIS HANDBOOK *Drs. Van Pelt, Ambrose, Newbold*	2.00
MODERN HYPNOSIS *Lesley Kuhn & Salvatore Russo, Ph.D.*	3.00
NEW CONCEPTS OF HYPNOSIS *Bernard C. Gindes, M.D.*	3.00
POST-HYPNOTIC INSTRUCTIONS *Arnold Furst*	2.00
How to give post-hypnotic suggestions for therapeutic purposes.	
PRACTICAL GUIDE TO SELF-HYPNOSIS *Melvin Powers*	2.00
PRACTICAL HYPNOTISM *Philip Magonet, M.D.*	1.00
SECRETS OF HYPNOTISM *S. J. Van Pelt, M.D.*	2.00
SELF-HYPNOSIS *Paul Adams*	2.00
SELF-HYPNOSIS Its Theory, Technique & Application *Melvin Powers*	2.00
SELF-HYPNOSIS A Conditioned-Response Technique *Laurance Sparks*	3.00
THERAPY THROUGH HYPNOSIS *edited by Raphael H. Rhodes*	3.00

JUDAICA

HOW TO LIVE A RICHER & FULLER LIFE *Rabbi Edgar F. Magnin*	2.00
MODERN ISRAEL *Lily Edelman*	2.00
OUR JEWISH HERITAGE *Rabbi Alfred Wolf & Joseph Gaer*	2.00
ROMANCE OF HASSIDISM *Jacob S. Minkin*	2.50
SERVICE OF THE HEART *Evelyn Garfield, Ph.D.*	3.00
STORY OF ISRAEL IN COINS *Jean & Maurice Gould*	2.00
STORY OF ISRAEL IN STAMPS *Maxim & Gabriel Shamir*	1.00
TONGUE OF THE PROPHETS *Robert St. John*	3.00
TREASURY OF COMFORT *edited by Rabbi Sidney Greenberg*	3.00

MARRIAGE, SEX & PARENTHOOD

METAPHYSICS & OCCULT

SELF-HELP & INSPIRATIONAL

____HOW TO DEVELOP A WINNING PERSONALITY *Martin Panzer*	2.00
____HOW TO DEVELOP AN EXCEPTIONAL MEMORY *Young & Gibson*	3.00
____HOW TO OVERCOME YOUR FEARS *M. P. Leahy, M.D.*	2.00
____HOW YOU CAN HAVE CONFIDENCE AND POWER *Les Giblin*	2.00
____I WILL *Ben Sweetland*	2.00
____LEFT-HANDED PEOPLE *Michael Barsley*	3.00
____MAGIC IN YOUR MIND *U. S. Andersen*	3.00
____MAGIC OF THINKING BIG *Dr. David J. Schwartz*	2.00
____MAGIC POWER OF YOUR MIND *Walter M. Germain*	3.00
____MENTAL POWER THRU SLEEP SUGGESTION *Melvin Powers*	1.00
____ORIENTAL SECRETS OF GRACEFUL LIVING *Boye De Mente*	1.00
____PRACTICAL GUIDE TO SUCCESS & POPULARITY *C. W. Bailey*	2.00
____PSYCHO-CYBERNETICS *Maxwell Maltz, M.D.*	2.00
____SECRET OF SECRETS *U. S. Andersen*	3.00
____STUTTERING AND WHAT YOU CAN DO ABOUT IT *W. Johnson, Ph.D.*	2.00
____SUCCESS-CYBERNETICS *U. S. Andersen*	2.00
____10 DAYS TO A GREAT NEW LIFE *William E. Edwards*	2.00
____THINK AND GROW RICH *Napoleon Hill*	3.00
____THREE MAGIC WORDS *U. S. Andersen*	3.00
____TREASURY OF THE ART OF LIVING *Sidney S. Greenberg*	3.00
____YOU ARE NOT THE TARGET *Laura Huxley*	3.00
____YOUR SUBCONSCIOUS POWER *Charles M. Simmons*	3.00

SPORTS

____ARCHERY — An Expert's Guide *Don Stamp*	2.00
____BICYCLING FOR FUN AND GOOD HEALTH *Kenneth E. Luther*	2.00
____CAMPING-OUT 101 Ideas & Activities *Bruno Knobel*	2.00
____COMPLETE GUIDE TO FISHING *Vlad Evanoff*	2.00
____HOW TO WIN AT POCKET BILLIARDS *Edward D. Knuchell*	3.00
____MOTORCYCLING FOR BEGINNERS *I. G. Edmonds*	2.00
____PRACTICAL BOATING *W. S. Kals*	3.00
____SECRET OF BOWLING STRIKES *Dawson Taylor*	2.00
____SECRET OF PERFECT PUTTING *Horton Smith & Dawson Taylor*	2.00
____SECRET WHY FISH BITE *James Westman*	2.00
____SKIER'S POCKET BOOK *Otti Wiedman* (4¼″ x 6″)	2.50
____TABLE TENNIS MADE EASY *Johnny Leach*	2.00

TENNIS LOVERS' LIBRARY

____BEGINNER'S GUIDE TO WINNING TENNIS *Helen Hull Jacobs*	2.00
____HOW TO BEAT BETTER TENNIS PLAYERS *Loring Fiske*	3.00
____HOW TO IMPROVE YOUR TENNIS—Style, Strategy & Analysis *C. Wilson*	2.00
____PSYCH YOURSELF TO BETTER TENNIS *Dr. Walter A. Luszki*	2.00
____TENNIS FOR BEGINNERS *Dr. H. A. Murray*	2.00
____TENNIS MADE EASY *Joel Brecheen*	2.00
____WEEKEND TENNIS—How to have fun & win at the same time *Bill Talbert*	2.00

WILSHIRE MINIATURE LIBRARY (4¼″ x 6″ in full color)

____BUTTERFLIES	2.50
____INTRODUCTION TO MINERALS	2.50
____LIPIZZANERS & THE SPANISH RIDING SCHOOL	2.50
____PRECIOUS STONES AND PEARLS	2.50
____SKIER'S POCKET BOOK	2.50

WILSHIRE PET LIBRARY

____DOG TRAINING MADE EASY & FUN *John W. Kellogg*	2.00
____HOW TO RAISE & TRAIN YOUR PUPPY *Jeff Griffen*	2.00
____PIGEONS: HOW TO RAISE & TRAIN THEM *William H. Allen, Jr.*	2.00

Notes

Notes

Notes

Notes

Notes

Notes

Notes

Notes